JARED POTTER KIRTLAND

Naturalist, Physician, Sage of the Western Reserve

Thomas M. Daniel

Sigel Press

Cleveland Museum of
NATURAL HISTORY

Sigel Press

4403 Belmont Court
Medina, Ohio 44256

51A Victoria Road
Cambridge CB4 3BW
England

Visit us on the World Wide Web at www.sigelpress.com.

Cover Design: Harp Mando. Image of Jared Potter Kirtland. Portrait painted in 1870 by Allen Smith, Jr. It now hangs in the Cleveland Museum of Natural History, on loan from Case Western Reserve University. Digital file is available at the archives of Case Western Reserve University. Reproduced with permission.

Internal Design: Harp Mando

Typesetting: Professional Book Compositors, Inc. Lorain, Ohio

ISBN: 978-1-905941-25-4

Printed in the United States of America

Printed on 100% recycled, post-consumer waste paper

FOR SCOTT R. INKLEY
FRIEND AND COLLEAGUE

Contents

Preface

Why Kirtland? Why did I choose to write a biography of Jared Potter Kirtland? Perhaps because he was one of the founders of and the first professor of medicine at the medical school where I spent my career as a professor of medicine. Perhaps because in my boyhood and youth I wanted to be naturalist; an early career goal was to be a National Park Service ranger. Perhaps because in my retirement years I developed a love of medical history, I was fascinated by the exhibits featuring Kirtland at the Dittrick Medical History Center museum. For some of these reasons or for all of them and more, I became intrigued with the life story of this eminent man about whom no book-length biography had been written. Over the several years I devoted to this project I became increasingly certain that Jared Potter Kirtland's story deserved to be told. It is my hope that I do him justice in this telling. In this book I recount many small happenings in Kirtland's life, often told in his letters, and I hope that in doing so I reveal the personality of this remarkable man.

Acknowledgments

Many people have helped with this book. It would not have been possible to assemble the material necessary to put together Kirtland's life story without the assistance of those who guard and preserve Kirtland's papers, books, and other materials. Let me first acknowledge the assistance of those individuals devoted to preserving historical materials, including in this instance materials related to Kirtland, at several archival repositories. They have been generous not only in giving me access to their institutions' collections, but also of their time and advice as I worked at their facilities. They include: at the Allen Medical Library of Case Western Reserve University, Debra Zabel, Reference Librarian, Dzwinka Holian, Librarian, and Christopher Dolwick, Library Assistant; at the Case Western Reserve University Archives, Helen Conger, Archivist, and Jill Tatem, Archivist; at The Cleveland Museum of Natural History, Carole Camillo, Registrar, Andy Jones, Ornithologist, and Wendy Wasman, Librarian and Archivist; at the Dittrick Medical History Center and Museum of Case Western Reserve University, James Edmonson, Chief Curator, Jennifer Nieves, Archivist, and Patsy Gerstner, Chief Curator Emerita; at the Hudson Library and Historical Society, Ellen Smith, Reference Librarian, and Gwen Mayer, Archivist; at the Kelvin Smith Library, Case Western Reserve University, Norma Sue Hanson, Librarian, Special Collections Research Center, Eleanor L. Blackman, Archivist, Special Collections Research Center, and Janet Klein, Librarian; at the Lakewood Historical Society, Amanda Francazio, Curator; at the Mahoning Valley Historical Society, Pamela Spies, Archivist, and Jessica Trickett, Curator; at Stetson University, DeLand, Florida, Susan M. Ryan, Associate Director, Dupont-Ball Library; at the Western Reserve Historical Society, Vicki Catozza, Archivist; and at Williams College, Williamstown, Massachusetts, Sylvia Kennick Brown, Archivist.

Although this is the first book-length published biography of Kirtland, others have written of him, and their efforts, as recovered from various repositories, have been enormously helpful in detailing Kirtland's life. I have cited them in notes as appropriate. Agnes Robbins Gehr wrote a master of arts thesis on Kirtland in 1950 for the Department of American Culture of Western Reserve University (now Case Western Reserve University). It was subsequently published with only minor revision in *The Explorer*, a publication of the Cleveland Museum of Natural History. Gehr's work is the most carefully researched and annotated previous biography of Kirtland available. Mae Ruth Smith wrote a much less comprehensive master of arts thesis for the Biology Department of Western Reserve University in 1934. Frederick Clayton Waite published many articles on the history of medicine and medical education in Northeast Ohio, including several on Kirtland. Margaret Manor Butler researched Kirtland's life with the intention of writing a biography of him, but never completed her project. Copies of her notes and other materials she collected are available at the Cleveland Museum of Natural History and the Lakewood Historical Society Museum. I consulted published materials relevant to Kirtland; I have cited them in my notes as appropriate.

Many individuals with knowledge relevant to Kirtland's life and the times in which he lived have generously given me time to discuss specific topics and aspects of Kirtland's life of which they had important knowledge. They include: Patsy Gerstner, the retired curator of the Dittrick Medical History Center; Lansing Hoskins, a friend, colleague, and lover of birds, and source of wisdom with respect to Brown-headed Thrushes and Kirtland's Warblers; Scott R. Inkley, a colleague and friend and longtime trustee of the Cleveland Museum of Natural History; David Marrs, a scholar with insights into American history; and Rebecca Rogers, a historian and horticulturist with an extensive knowledge of Kirtland's Poland years.

Finally, several individuals have read parts or all of drafts of my manuscript. They have found my errors and made corrections that have immeasurably improved this work. First among them is Janet Daniel, my wife, who has read through multiple drafts as the work has progressed. Her eagle eye for typographic and grammatical errors has been invaluable to me. Moreover, she made insightful comments about the content of this biography. Others who have critiqued my manuscript include: Patricia Eldredge, Scott R. Inkley, Joe Hannibal, Rebecca Rogers, Wendy Wasman, and Harvey Webster.

My thanks and gratitude go to Sarah Riehl, who has skillfully and diligently edited my manuscript. Her careful work has greatly improved my text. I also thank Harp Mando who created the internal book and cover design; Professional Book Compositors for typesetting the book; and Thomas Sigel, the publisher of Sigel Press for overseeing production of this book.

Generous grants supporting the publication of this work were made to the Cleveland Museum of Natural History by the Kent H. Smith Charitable Trust and the Elizabeth Ring Mather and William Gwinn Mather Fund. The author and the museum are grateful to these donors for their generosity. They made this book possible.

1

Pigs, Flowers, a Horse, and a Bird

It was a hot summer day in Rockport, Ohio. Dirt from the soil of the farm he loved was on his hands as Jared Potter Kirtland stood in a sty feeding his pigs. The pail of slops to be fed to the porkers was at the roadside on the other side of a fence. A young man approached walking on the dirt road. "Would you be kind enough to hand that pail over to me?" asked Kirtland. He did so, and Kirtland thanked him. "But I don't know you," he added.

"Reverend Mercer, pastor of the Swedenborgian Church."

"Well, you should be wearing a tall hat and a tail coat for that profession."[1]

Writing for the *Cleveland Plain Dealer* in 1931, Ella Grant Wilson reflected on her encounter with Kirtland.

> Early in my business career I drove in a buggy to get my flower supplies.... Mr. Thorpe asked me how far I was going. I told him to Rockport....
>
> Would I take a letter out to Dr. Kirtland, he asked, and as I had always wanted to meet Dr. Kirtland I readily agreed....
>
> On arriving at the home of Dr. Kirtland, I entered the grounds and went around to the side door. Here I found an old gentleman with a bushy shock of white hair seated in the shade of a tree. I inquired of him where I could find Dr. Kirtland.
>
> "I don't think you will have to go far to find him, and he looked at me with a twinkle in his eye. I dropped to the situa-

tion that this must be the renowned Dr. Kirtland, so I handed him the letter.

He said, "Well ... you might as well sit down and be comfortable." So I sat near him while he read the communication. Then he turned to me with a chuckle and said, "Mr. Thorpe says you are interested in flowers. That is a good thing to be interested in. Want to see mine?"

So we strolled over to his flower border, which was a straight line on both sides of a walk.[2]

Kirtland's reputation as a naturalist was well-established nationally and his articles were being read at eastern universities. A distinguished scholar made the arduous coach journey from the East Coast to Rockport (what is today Lakewood) to visit Kirtland. Kirtland's pioneering work on molluscs had appeared in the *American Journal of Science and Arts*, America's first scientific journal, which was edited and published by Professor Benjamin Silliman at Yale. Seeing a man working on the grounds in front of Kirtland's house, the visitor asked him to hold his horse. The man graciously obliged. The visitor went to the front door of the handsome house, where he was greeted by Mary Pease, Kirtland's daughter. "Is the doctor in?" asked the visitor.

"Oh, yes, he's out there holding someone's horse."[3]

On May 13, 1851, Kirtland's son-in-law, Charles Pease, shot a previously unknown bird on Kirtland's Rockport farm.[4] Kirtland showed the specimen to Spencer Fullerton Baird, curator of the Smithsonian Institution. Baird, an expert ornithologist, and Kirtland were friends. They had returned together from attending a meeting of the recently founded American Association for the Advancement of Science in Cincinnati, Ohio, and Baird was visiting Kirtland at his home. They were making plans for the next meeting of the association, which they hoped might be held in Cleveland. Baird named the new bird species *Sylvicola kirtlandii* (later renamed *Dendroica kirtlandii*), honoring his host. Today bird-watchers travel to stands of young jack pines in the upper part of

Michigan's Lower Peninsula to see this rare warbler. In recent years, however, Kirtland's Warblers migrating between their Bahamian wintering grounds and their Michigan nesting sites have been seen near the shores of Lake Erie.

The stories about the pigs and the horse are apocryphal. The account of the naming of Kirtland's Warbler is well documented, as is that of Ms. Wilson's visit. All four of these brief accounts provide insightful portraits of this man of modest demeanor and enormous intellect.

Tall and large of stature, physically imposing, spectacles often pushed back on his head, Jared Potter Kirtland was a distinguished naturalist, a professor of medicine, and a notable and public-spirited citizen. He was one of the founders of what is now Case Western Reserve University School of Medicine. He was a member of the nation's most august scientific societies. Yet he was at his core a modest man, a man of the people. He was a liberal thinker and an abolitionist. He valued money only as a means to an end, not as a source of personal enrichment. As years passed, his interests increasingly focused on natural history and his farm and orchard, although he never forgot medicine. During his life, Kirtland became known as "The Sage of Rockport." A sage he was. Loved and respected by his neighbors, his reputation and influence extended far beyond Rockport.

2

Puritan Origins

P rotestants who rejected the Roman pope and his authority emerged in Europe during the early sixteenth century. On October 31, 1517, Martin Luther posted his famous theses protesting the sale of indulgences on the door of his church in Wittenberg. Anabaptists appeared in Germany shortly thereafter; they soon became known as Moravians. In 1531 Henry VIII wrested control of the church in England away from the pope and his cardinals. Five years later the English parliament stripped the pope of authority in England. In 1541 John Knox established Presbyterianism in Scotland. Within this remarkable quarter-century, religious beliefs and practices in Europe were forever changed.

Calvinism swept Europe following the publication of *Institutes of Christian Religion* by John Calvin in 1536. Calvin rejected much of the liturgy and ritual of Catholicism and promoted a stern, uncompromising approach to God; God alone could offer salvation. Many Protestant sects and denominations had their origins in Calvinism. Notable among them were the Puritans, most of whom lived in southeastern England. As a cohesive, emerging Protestant denomination, they had their beginnings in about 1560; the designation "Puritan" began to be used at about that time. As they grew in number, the Puritans sought separation from the established Church of England. They migrated in large numbers to New England, the first group famously on the *Mayflower* in 1620. There they established what was essentially a Calvinist theocratic state.

In 1629 Puritans in Salem, Massachusetts, stated their faith in the Salem Covenant:

We covenant with the Lord and one another; and do bind
ourselves in the presence of God, to walk together in all his
ways, according as he is pleased to reveal himself unto us in
his Blessed word of truth.

Thus they united themselves, allowing none of the individuality of be-
lief now cherished by the congregations of their descendants, who worship in churches of the United Church of Christ, formerly the
Congregational Church.

Although large numbers of Puritans left England, it is incorrect to
assume that they left seeking independence from British rule. For the
most part, they considered themselves English subjects, and they viewed
their emigration as removal to British colonies, not to new nations. What
they sought in leaving their homeland was a new religious environment,
not political autonomy. It would be another century and a half before
the American Revolution would erupt.

Jared Potter Kirtland's forebears were Puritans. Kirtland had an interest in his genealogy, and handwritten transcriptions of his notes about
his paternal ancestry have been preserved at the Mahoning Valley Historical Society in Youngstown, Ohio. They are, unfortunately, faded to
the point where they can no longer be read. However, in 1871 one of
his descendants copied them, and that copy remains legible. Also in the
same archive are handwritten notes in a book entitled *Family Record*. The
date and authorship of these notes is unknown, but they all appear to
have been written by one hand.[1] Figure 2.1 presents a family tree of Jared
Potter Kirtland's direct ancestral lineage.

The Kirtland name may be Scottish, although no Scottish ancestors
are known. In fact *Kirtland*, which has many variants, is not commonly
found in English archives. It is spelled Kyrtland in a number of early
genealogical records, including the Kirtland family's records, and was
probably used in that form by Kirtland's ancestors prior to their emigration to New England, as well as by the first immigrants in the family during their early years in New England. The name may be a variant
of Curtland, indicating a lack of land holdings. Kirkland, another possible variant, is of English rather than Scottish origin. It was most commonly found in Sussex and Derbyshire Counties.

The earliest traceable ancestor was named John; nothing more is
known of him. John's son, John Kyrtland, was born about 1580. He and

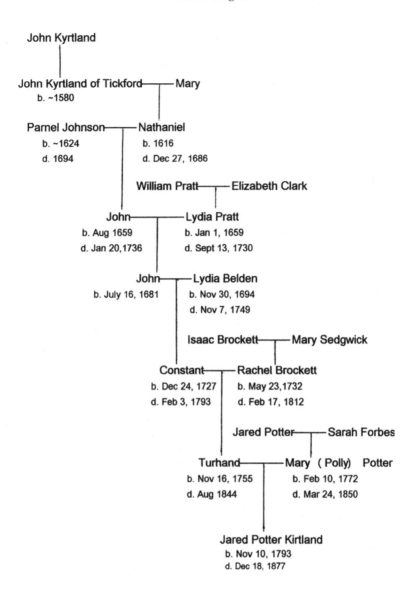

Figure 2.1. Kirtland Family Tree. The family can be traced back to Puritans in the early seventeenth century. In compiling this geneaological tree, precedence has been given to dates and spellings used by Jared Potter Kirtland and his descendants, which sometimes vary from those in published sources.[2]

his wife, Mary, lived in Tickford in Buckinghamshire in Southeastern England. John Kyrtland wrote a will dated 12 December 1616. The will names seven children. Not all were necessarily his offspring; some may have been his nephews and nieces.

The two oldest Kyrtland sons, Nathaniel and Philip, born in about 1616 and 1614 respectively, sailed to New England aboard the *Hopewell* in April 1635. Her master was William Bundocke. On the ship's manifest the brothers' names were spelled Kyrtland and their residence given as Sherrington in Buckinghamshire. It was in this part of England that the Puritan movement was strongest, and the Kyrtlands probably practiced this form of Calvinist Protestant Christianity. Many of their sixty-six fellow passengers also came from Buckinghamshire.

The *Hopewell* was making its second voyage of the year carrying Puritans to the New World. In fact, it was part of a large fleet of vessels plying the route to New England. These immigrant settlers of the new land followed their Calvin-inspired religious faith. They accepted without challenge a way of life based in their understanding of Christianity. To the Puritans, and hence probably to Nathaniel and Philip Kyrtland, New England represented a way to live in what they believed to be God's way.[3] During the weeks of what was often a stormy Atlantic crossing, the group's leaders preached sermons, often several times a day, extolling the virtues of the Puritan approach to God. Their faith was to be strengthened.

It is incorrect to assume that religious beliefs were the sole motivation leading the Kyrtland brothers to join other Puritans in sailing for New England. In fact, there is no documentation that they were Puritans, although it seems probable. During the eleven years from 1629 to 1640, Charles I ruled England without convening parliament. At the same time, Anglican Archbishop William Laud attempted to rid the established church of all Puritans. In addition, it was a time of economic depression. During that brief period of English history about 80,000 Englishmen and their families left their homeland. Some went to Ireland, some to the Netherlands, some to the Caribbean. More than 20,000 sailed for Massachusetts. While many were Puritans, many others wished only to escape a time of privation in England. Were economic rather than religious factors behind the emigration of the Kyrtland brothers? Their subsequent actions would suggest not, but that they were among Puritans motivated by their religious beliefs. This great migration to the New World ended abruptly in 1640.[4]

The path ahead for all Puritan believers was clear and predestined. John Winthrop, a leader in the Massachusetts Bay Colony, preached to his fellow pilgrims:

> Wee shall be as a City upon a Hill, the eies of all people are upon us; soe that if wee shall deale falsely with our god in this worke wee have undertaken and soe cause him to withdrawe his present help from us, we shall be made a story and by-word through the worlds.[5]

American children are told every autumn at Thanksgiving time that the Pilgrims sailed to America seeking religious freedom. The Puritans were devout, and they sought separation from the established worship and governance of the Church of England. However, their religious life was far from free; it was rigidly controlled and highly structured. The sermons of their religious leaders guided every aspect of not only their relations with God but also of their daily lives. There was no room for dissent. Those who found themselves uncomfortable in the new Puritan colony moved on to another location.

The *Hopewell* made land at Salem, Massachusetts, a favorable port north of Boston, which did not then provide a good harbor. The Kyrtland brothers settled initially in Lynn, a few miles south of Salem. Philip became a shoemaker in Lynn. He bought property. Nathaniel had no trade and did not acquire land. He was a husbandman, that is, a farmer. He probably sought employment as a farmhand, perhaps working for his brother. Many, even most, of those who boarded ships for the New World came as families, and the men were usually traders or craftsmen. They were generally well-off, accustomed to earning a comfortable living at a trade. Pursuing these trades was often difficult and unrewarding in New England; it was the farmers who prospered.[6]

Nathaniel Kirtland may have strayed somewhat from the rigorous dicta of the Puritans—restless, perhaps. On June 25, 1667, at a time when he had been in the New World some three decades, his brother testified in connection with a suit brought by one Isaack Disberoc, that "Nathanyell Kartland ... used to come into Mr. Croft's house upon the Lord's Day when his master was at meeting, roasting apples and drinking cider."[7]

Nathaniel Kirtland went to Long Island, probably accompanied initially by his brother, and settled in Southold at the northeastern tip of the island. Neither the date nor the circumstances of this move are known. Southold was founded in 1646 by John Yonges, a Puritan minister who had arrived in New England in 1637.[8] On Long Island, Nathaniel Kirtland met twenty-eight-year-old Parnel Johnson. They were married in 1652; the marriage took place in Southampton, Long Island. Born in England in about 1624, she was a Puritan, and her influence probably shaped his life. She outlived him, and after his death wrote a will in which she directed her executor to withhold inheritance from any of her heirs who had espoused "Quakerism or other apostasies."

If Nathaniel Kirtland's move was occasioned by dissent rather than simply a need to move on to another opportunity, he must have reconciled his difference with the Massachusetts Puritans, for he returned to Lynn some time before 1658. He became a notable citizen and a property owner, perhaps an investor in land. In October 1663 he sold a "dwelling house and two acres to Joseph Armitage, a tailor."[9] He was elected a selectman in that community in 1673, serving from June of that year to November 1678. His health failed shortly thereafter. On November 30, 1680, Sergeant Kirtland was fined for failing to appear to serve on a grand jury. He was then excused and the fine remitted on account of "weakness and inability."[10] Nathaniel Kirtland died in Lynn on December 27, 1686, at the age of seventy.

Nathaniel and Parnel had eight children. Their fourth child, a son named John, was born in Lynn in August 1659. He grew to become a blacksmith. Like many of his contemporaries, he was called into the militia, and he served in skirmishes against Native Americans. Chosen to be a lieutenant, he commanded the fort at Saybrook Point at the mouth of the Connecticut River on the Long Island Sound shore.

John Kirtland was one of the twenty-four proprietors (property owners) of newly founded Saybrook and served as both constable and selectman. He married Lydia Pratt, the daughter of Lieutenant William Pratt and his wife, Elisabeth Clark Pratt, on November 18, 1679. They settled in Saybrook and had a son, John, who was born on July 16, 1681, the first of ten children. John (the younger) married Temperance Buckingham in March of 1702 or 1703. They had three children before she died. He then married Lydia Belden on August 22, 1716. They had nine children, two of whom died in infancy and two others as young children. Their son, Constant Kirtland, was born in Saybrook on December 24, 1727. He was the second son named Constant, the first having died in infancy a year earlier.

Constant Kirtland left Saybrook as a youth to learn the trade of carriage-making from William Ward of Wallingford, Connecticut. Kirtland married Rachel Brockett on April 19, 1753, and settled in Wallingford, building a house at Pond Hill. Rachel was the daughter of Isaac Brockett and Mary Sedgwick Brockett. The *Kirtland Family Notes* describes her as of "royal lineage." Their son, Turhand Kirtland, was born two years later.

As a young man, Turhand Kirtland served in Washington's army during the American Revolution, as did many of the men of his generation. The Connecticut Land Company, new owners of the vast Western Reserve in Northeast Ohio, held a lottery to apportion those holdings to its investors. Caleb Atwater, representing a group that included Kirtland, drew land in the present townships of Poland, Burton, and Kirtland.[11]

The Connecticut Land Company chose Turhand Kirtland to be their resident agent in the area in 1797.[12] One of the original proprietors of the Connecticut Land Company, he was then forty-two years old.

A widower, Turhand had married again in early 1793 (it was common for widowers to remarry). His second wife, Mary Potter, called Polly, had been born in Wallingford on February 10, 1772. She was the daughter of Jared Potter, a doctor in Wallingford, Connecticut, and Sarah Forbes Potter. Potter had served as a surgeon with a Connecticut regiment during the American Revolution, seeing action along Lakes George and Champlain in Upstate New York.

The couple's first child had been born on November 10, 1793. They named him Jared Potter Kirtland in honor of Polly's father. Five other children would follow.[13]

Just four years after his oldest child's birth, Turhand set out for the new domain of the Western Reserve, crossing New York State to the Great Lakes. Upon arriving on June 3, 1798, he made camp on the bank of the Grand River at a point about three miles from its mouth on Lake Erie. From there, he and the surveyors who accompanied him cut a road through the eastern regions of the Western Reserve to Burton and then to the village of Poland. He visited early settlers and identified township borders along the way. He established his headquarters in Poland, close to the Pennsylvania border, just south of present-day Youngstown. It was at this southeast corner of the Western Reserve that the survey of the region and its division into ranges and townships began. For the next five years, Kirtland traveled back and forth between his home in Connecticut and the new frontier. In 1803 he journeyed west to settle permanently with his wife and family in Poland. Jared

Potter Kirtland was ten years old when his parents and siblings moved to Poland. He remained in Connecticut with his physician grandfather, the better to further his education.

Turhand Kirtland not only served as land agent, he also became a leading citizen of the new land.[14] Together with John Young, he laid out the village of Poland. He became an associate judge. In that role he oversaw the conviction of two settlers who had murdered two Indians. He was one of the nine "corporators" of the Western Reserve Bank, which was chartered in the winter of 1811-1812 with $100,000 capital. It was one of the first banks chartered in Ohio, and perhaps the only one to remain solvent throughout its existence until it was liquidated in 1866. Twenty of the initial shares, worth $500, were assigned to his son Jared. Turhand Kirtland was a senator in the legislature of the young State of Ohio in 1814.[15] Upon its founding in 1826, he became a trustee of Western Reserve College in Hudson.

Life in the early years of the Western Reserve could be challenging. Years later, when Jared Potter Kirtland was invited to attend a historical celebration of Mahoning County (location of Poland) he declined because of his advanced age. In his letter of regret sent from East Rockport (now Lakewood), Ohio, on August 29, 1874, he described an incident in Turhand Kirtland's life in Poland.

> On August 23rd Turhand Kirtland had partially recovered from an attack of fever and ague. He went from Poland to Youngstown to get his horse shod; was required to blow and strike for the smith. This threw him into an aggravated relapse of the disorder, which was at length cured by taking teaspoonful doses of the bark every hour.[16]

This fever and ague was probably malaria, which was prevalent throughout North America at that time; the bark was likely the quinine-containing bark of the Peruvian cinchona tree.

Though the Kirtland family had Puritans in its ancestry, it is not clear through how many generations that religious practice held. From its earliest days, the Western Reserve had many Congregational churches that traced their lineage to the New England Puritans. Yet both Turhand and Polly were Episcopalians and founding members of Poland's first Episcopal Church. They were buried in the Presbyterian cemetery, the only cemetery in Poland at that time.

3

The Western Reserve

Woody Guthrie sang, "This land is your land, this land is my land." "We know we belong to the land," is the choral refrain in Richard Rodgers and Oscar Hammerstein's "Oklahoma." Surely, the land in which we live shapes each of us. Surely, if we are to know Jared Potter Kirtland we must know the land in which he lived. His land was the Western Reserve of Connecticut.

When the first British settlers established their seventeenth-century outposts on the Atlantic shores of North America, they had no knowledge and only vague concepts of the size of the continent upon which they settled. As they organized themselves into political units they attempted to define their colonial borders, often finding themselves in conflict with their neighbors. The British crown gave patents to its colonies, but these often overlapped and were usually vaguely worded. And there was no understanding of the westward reaches of the land.

The borders of Connecticut were set in 1630 by a royal conveyance that defined its northern border at two minutes north of the forty-second parallel. The southern border was defined by Long Island Sound, with the state then being bounded by Massachusetts on the north, and Rhode Island and New York on the east and west. Western expansion, which all of the colonies viewed as their destiny, was not available to the citizens of Connecticut. In 1662 King Charles II of England offered a measure of relief. He granted to Connecticut the lands between the forty-first and forty-second parallels extending the unimagined distance from Pennsylvania westward to the Pacific Ocean—the Southern Sea, as it was then called. Ever generous, however, Charles II gave much of the same land to New York and to William Penn for Pennsylvania. Moreover, Virginia claimed some of the region. The borders of Pennsylvania were not yet established at this time, however, and many citizens of Connecticut had settled in the Wyoming Valley of the Susquehanna River.

During the mid-eighteenth century the competing claims of Connecticut and Pennsylvania led to petitions to the British crown, and Charles II responded with conflicting grants that further confused the entitlements of the two colonies. With the outbreak of the American Revolution, the citizens of Connecticut set aside thoughts of westward expansion. They were resumed at the end of the war, and in 1784 Connecticut relinquished its claims in the Wyoming Valley to Pennsylvania, claiming for itself land extending 120 miles west of Pennsylvania. Asserting its claims on the basis of the 1662 grant from Charles II, Connecticut "reserved" the area in a Deed of Cession on September 13, 1786. It was the southern shore of Lake Erie, however, and not the forty-second parallel that would define the northern border of what became known as the Western Reserve of Connecticut.[1]

Not all claims to what became the Western Reserve originated with the English colonists in Connecticut. Even before the arrival of the *Mayflower* at Plymouth Rock in 1620, King James I had issued grants to colonists in 1606, 1609, and 1611 that Connecticut would later aver justified its claim to these lands. In 1669 and 1670 René-Robert Cavelier, Sieur de La Salle, explored the region and claimed it for France. When the French-Indian War ended with the Treaty of Paris on February 10, 1763, the "Great West" was ceded by France to England. The Americans took control of what became known as the "Northwest Territory" by another treaty signed in Paris on September 3, 1783. Benjamin Franklin had already noted the potential of this region, calling it "the great country back of the Appalachian mountains" in a paper written in 1755.[2]

By the mid-eighteenth century, a few pioneering settlers from New England were making their way into what became known as the Northwest to establish small communities and farm the rich soils of the region. This push to the west was increasingly chaotic and was evidently of concern to the Confederation Congress of 1785. Pressure for laws regulating the ownership and sale of western lands was great. Thus, on May 20, 1785, this legislative body enacted a Land Ordinance and, on July 13, 1787, a second land law, the Northwest Land Ordinance.

These laws regulated property ownership, but they did more than that; they promoted education. Schools, colleges, and universities were rapidly being established in New England, and those who looked westward wanted similar educational institutions to flourish there. The 1785 law required that lot number 16 of every newly surveyed township be set aside for the support of public schools within that township. Perhaps a school might be located on that lot; perhaps rent from that township might be used to support a school elsewhere. Citizens of Connecticut who migrated to the Western Reserve expected to have education available to their children. The Northwest Ordinance of 1787 was one of the early nation's most important legislative acts. It set the terms under which new states could join the union. It prohibited slavery north of the Ohio River. It further fostered education and was fundamental in establishing future state university systems.

As noted, New York, Massachusetts, and Virginia all had claims to portions of the land across the mountains, and these claims conflicted with that of Connecticut. A compromise reached in 1786 led Connecticut to cede to the nascent federal government all of its "right, title, interest, jurisdiction, and claim" beyond the strip north of the forty-first parallel extending120 miles from the Pennsylvania border to Maumee Bay at the western end of Lake Erie. This 3.5 million-acre strip of land became Connecticut's Western Reserve.[3]

During the American Revolution, British troops had pillaged and burned many of the settlements along the Long Island Sound shore of Connecticut. In May 1792, the General Assembly of Connecticut set aside the westernmost 25 miles of the Western Reserve, comprising a half million acres, for the benefit of the inhabitants of nine Connecticut towns that had been hard-hit by the British soldiers. Known as the Fire Sufferers' Lands, or Firelands, it now comprises Ohio's Erie and Huron Counties. The name "Firelands" remains in frequent use in the area. More than 1,800 claims were settled by awarding land in this area. The Firelands were thus separated from the Western Reserve, although they also owed their origins to Connecticut.

Securely in possession of their Western Reserve, the citizens of Connecticut faced the issue of how to handle its disposition. High on their list of priorities was reaping money for education systems within the state. In October 1786 the General Assembly of Connecticut passed legislation authorizing survey and sale of land in the Western Reserve, but nothing was done to implement these actions.

Several years passed, and in 1795 the assembly devised a plan that was welcomed by the citizenry. A representative from each of Connecticut's eight counties formed a committee charged with selling the land for a total price of not less than $1 million. The proceeds were to be placed in an endowment fund, the income of which was to be used for the support of schools in Connecticut. This sale was accomplished on September 2, 1795, for $1.2 million to the Connecticut Land Company.

In fact, this so-called company was not an incorporated entity. It was a loosely organized group of thirty-five men, called proprietors, interested in land speculation. They conducted a lottery, called a draft, each drawing lots for acreage related to the amount of money he was willing to invest. After the sale, this agency drew up articles of association spelling out its future operations. It would conduct surveys, develop the region, and sell land to return profit to its proprietors.[4]

In 1796 the Connecticut Land Company dispatched a survey team headed by Moses Cleaveland to the Western Reserve. Cleaveland was a leading citizen of Connecticut. He was a big man, stocky, and dark-complected. A 1777 Yale graduate, a lawyer practicing in the new state for thirty years, and a general in the state militia, he had served several terms in the state legislature. Prosperous, he had subscribed for land in the Western Reserve in the amount of $32,600.[5] With his party of surveyors and support personnel—some fifty people in all—he set out in May on what became an arduous journey that served up more privations than pleasures.[6]

June found the travelers near Buffalo, New York, and there they met with representatives of six Iroquois nations to settle still-unresolved territorial issues. After three days of negotiations and ceremony, accompanied by the giving of gifts and $1,500 to the Iroquois men, a treaty was concluded that gave the land east of the Cuyahoga River to the Connecticut Land Company; the western half of the Western Reserve would be a source of friction with Native Americans for many years.

The western border of Pennsylvania had been surveyed some ten years earlier. A broad swath had been cut through the forest along the border, and stakes placed to mark it. Sixty-eight days after departing from Connecticut, Cleaveland and his party reached the northwest corner of

Pennsylvania and entered the Western Reserve. They made camp on a point beside the mouth of Conneaut Creek at Lake Erie. They named this camp Fort Independence. Seth Pease, third in command of the party and a surveyor and astronomer, found the clearly marked surveyor's stake denoting the border between Pennsylvania and the Western Reserve of Connecticut.

It was July 4, 1796. A time and place for celebration. The men of the military contingent in the party raised their rifles and fired a salute. Grog was passed, and toasts offered to the president of the United States (John Adams) and to the Connecticut Land Company. Three cheers were raised, and then the group feasted and continued the celebration with more grog. Negotiations with local members of the Massasagoes Indians followed the next day, which reaffirmed the treaty negotiated in Buffalo. Then the party moved on further westward along the Lake Erie shore.

On July 22, Cleaveland and his party reached the mouth of the Cuyahoga River (the name comes from the Iroquois and means "crooked river"). There they established a settlement. Surprising him, his men named the new town that he laid out Cleaveland (now Cleveland), an honor that he was pleased to receive. Cleaveland's surveyors completed their work at the end of September. Cleaveland returned to Connecticut, never again to visit the Western Reserve.

Seth Pease was the principal surveyor for the Connecticut Land Company's exploratory party. He knew his trade and was also a competent astronomer, which helped in determining latitudes. Pease and his men set out from Conneaut to follow the Pennsylvania border south to the forty-first parallel.[7] Measuring carefully with their rods and chains, they followed a path about thirty feet west of the marked Pennsylvania border. Two weeks were required to make the nearly sixty-eight-mile traverse. At times their route crossed swamps, which proved difficult for the horses carrying their supplies. Mosquitoes tormented them. They met and crossed a beaver pond. They were sometimes short of food. On July 21 the party reached the forty-first parallel, confirming their location astronomically by sighting the North Star. There they erected a chestnut marker post. Pease rejoined Cleaveland's party at the mouth of the Cuyahoga River and took charge of laying out the nascent village of Cleaveland on the east bank of the river. With other members of the party, he retired to Connecticut in October.

Pease went back to the Western Reserve the following year as the principal surveyor in a nine-member party that surveyed and laid out all of the ranges and townships between the Pennsylvania border and the Cuyahoga River. Ranges were set at five miles, east to west, township lines at five miles, south to north. Thus, each township comprised twenty-five square miles. Early in 1798 Pease completed a map based on his work, which was engraved that spring. Five hundred copies were printed.[8] There were a number of difficulties in precisely locating the corners of the Western Reserve, resulting in some irregularities in township borders. In fact, the first surveyor's stake on the Pennsylvania border in Poland was placed one-half mile south of the forty-first parallel. When the line reached the point 120 miles west at the western border of the Western Reserve, it was correctly sited on the forty-first parallel. Thus, the southern border was skewed.

In 1807 Pease returned to the Western Reserve as the head of yet another team of surveyors. Native American claims to territory east of the Cuyahoga River had been resolved by the Treaty of Fort Industry in 1805. Joined by William Tappen, Pease completed a survey mapping the entire territory. They corrected earlier errors, and a second, more accurate map, known as the Pease-Tappen map, was published in 1808. On this map names were assigned to most of the sixty-seven townships, generally reflecting their ownership. Tappen conducted additional surveys together with Amos Ruggles. At meetings in Turhand Kirtland's home in Poland, many discrepancies were resolved, allowing assignments of property lines. Not until late the following year were all of the problems resolved by further surveys carried out by Ruggles.

Shortly after Pease initiated his original surveys of the Western Reserve, Turhand Kirtland traveled to Poland in Range 1, Township 1 at the southeast corner of the region to establish his land office. The trip was made in the company of other settlers, most headed for Cleveland. In the draft of the Connecticut Land Company, Turhand Kirtland had drawn allotments in the Western Reserve in partnerships with several others. As a result he held title to property in townships that now include Kirtland, Auburn, Mecca, and Burton, as well as Poland. However, given his role as land agent, Poland seemed to be the appropriate place for Kirtland to settle.

Turhand Kirtland kept a diary during his journey to Poland. This diary survives.[9] It provides an interesting account of his first trip there and insights into life in the Western Reserve at the end of the eighteenth century. Leaving their homes in Connecticut, he and his companions took a route that crossed New York state, passing through Albany and towns at the heads of the Finger Lakes. On May 12, 1798, they crossed the Genesee River "with oxen, two cows, one steer, having in company forty head of cattle and wine. Spent two nights in the woods, ... leaving the cattle with the men to come on next morning." Thereafter, they traveled to the mouth of the Niagara River.

At daylight [on Sunday, May 20] we went up the river to Queenstown, but having a large number of Canadian boats arrived the day before us, was detained at the portage until Tuesday noon. When[ce] I arrived at Chippeway and proceeded to Fort Erie, which lies on the north side of the river at the outlet of the lake, about three miles from Buffalo.

On Saturday, June 3, 1798, he and his party entered the Grand River at its mouth on Lake Erie. Other travelers bound for Cleveland left Kirtland's party at that point. Kirtland and his group traveled up the river a short distance before making camp for the night. There they found "as fine large strawberries as ever I saw." Three days later near an Indian settlement they began the arduous task of cutting a road to Poland. Progress was slow, as they had to cut through hardwood forests. They started from a point four miles up the river from its mouth and on the first day accomplished about two miles. On June 7 Kirtland noted, "Moved on a small distance, broke our sled. Esq. Law went back after tools. Mended our sled and cut on about two miles, being much obstructed by swamps, etc." A few days later they were hindered by rain. "June 12 — Heavy thunder and ... rain.... Made our way on ... about two and one-half miles, being in lot No. 2, Town 9 in Range 8 (Chardon), having traveled all day as wet as water could make us."

On June 15 the party reached Range 7, Township 7, where a man named Burton had settled. Kirtland took time to explore the township a bit. He thought the quality of the land "very good," with "timber large:

Chestnut, Black Walnut, hickory, oak, Maple, ash, whitewood, and some beach [sic], plenty of stone and good water." His party camped by the side of "an excellent spring and a warm excellent place for a garden."

Spring rains in Northeast Ohio continued well into June, and they often encumbered the surveying party. A diary entry on June 23 recorded:

> This morning Mr. Beard [a lead surveyor] and his men come in to breakfast very wet, having lain out in the woods all night; very rainy, without any tent,—took breakfast.— The weather cleared up, they went out again to run the fifth line east and west.

Indeed, rains followed Kirtland and his men, drenching them and slowing work every few days. On June 30 Beard and his survey crew were again "hindered by rain and swamp." Kirtland described the weather as "very hot with showers."

Food for the party came from the forest. On June 22, "we caught a very fine fawn we judged to be about one month old, which made us an excellent dinner." Three days later and again on the move, they had quite a different dinner. "Being out of bread and flour," the party found itself looking for food. "[We] killed a large rattle snake—fifteen rattles— and ... cooked him. Notwithstanding my exclamations to the contrary, after it was cook, it was generally eat with as good a relish as any fresh meat we had on the road."

Illness visited the survey party. Kirtland noted in his diary the indisposition of various members of the team. For five days in early August he was disabled by diarrhea. He took a "physic"; one wonders if this medicine might have been the Potter's Powders, a remedy for intestinal illness developed by his father-in-law, Dr. Jared Potter (Chapter 4).

Slowly they pushed on. They spent several weeks surveying lots within the region traversed by the new road that they cut. On August 26 Kirtland set out for Poland. He reached Young's Town on August 27, where he was able to get his horse shod. Two days later, Turhand Kirtland reached Poland, where he joined two members of his party who had gone ahead. There he set about building a cabin for himself. He also took up his duties as land agent, selling parcels to several individuals. In Poland, Kirtland joined his brother-in-law, Jonathan Fowler, who had married Lydia Kirtland, Turhand's sister. The Fowlers and their infant were the first settlers from Connecticut in Poland, preceding Turhand Kirtland by one year. Fowler opened Poland's first saw and grist mills in 1801. On October 11 Kirtland set out for "home" in Connecticut, traveling overland through Pittsburgh. He would return the following year.

Kirtland's diary entry from Poland on Thursday, October 11, 1798, notes the taxes levied to pay the costs of his surveying and road-building efforts.

The tax voted by the company at Wallingford
for to defray the expense of surveying of
1798 was $35 to each $1000 in the
original purchase. Turhand Kirtland share
[in the original purchase] was $4750 $166.25
Jan 1, 1799, at New Haven, voted a tax of
$20 on each $1,000 of original purchase   95.00

                                          $261.25

Voted a tax of one cent on the acre for road   47.50
Voted one cent of the dollar for Mills, Towns, etc.

Kirtland would be reimbursed and paid for his travails, but he would also be taxed as one of the proprietors.

They were hardy souls, those who ventured to claim holdings in the newly surveyed Western Reserve. A few men who had been early traders in the region settled there. Some adventurous individuals had moved into the area as early as ten years before the establishment of the Western Reserve and the subsequent surveys. Most of the members of the original surveying parties did not return. Gradually, those who had acquired land in the Connecticut Land Company's draft came into the region with their families. For the most part they sought farmland. Cleveland, on the shore of Lake Erie, served for water access, but was not considered a place to reside. Homes were widely dispersed, isolated, or in small communities of only a few residents.

In the original draft held in Connecticut, Ephraim Kirby and two or three other residents of Litchfield obtained a deed entitling them to one-twentieth of the region.[10] David Hudson Jr. paid them $1,500 on October 10, 1795, for the rights to 3,000 acres of their holding. At the time of these transactions, the survey had not been conducted, and Hudson's rights entitled him to an amount of land rather than a specific tract. Following the completion of Pease's surveys and the establishment of ranges and townships, Hudson found himself the owner of the entirety of Township 4 in Range 10, five square miles, 3,200 acres. The story of his move to the Western Reserve to take possession of his land is representative of the travails of many of those who were early settlers there.[11]

David Hudson Jr. was born on February 17, 1761, in Goshen, Connecticut. His father owned a prosperous farm, and the young man began life as a farmer. On December 23, 1783, he married Anna Norton. He built a substantial house on the family farm. Soon the couple began a family. They would ultimately have eight children, the last born in their new home in what would become the village of Hudson in the Western Reserve.

On April 22, 1799, Hudson set out for his new land. He took with him his eleven-year-old son, Ira, leaving his older son, Samuel, who was mentally disabled, and four other children with Anna in Goshen. He hired two local men to accompany him. Additional men joined the party along the way. On his journey, Hudson met Benjamin Tappan, also bound for the Western Reserve. The two men consolidated their parties. They sent their livestock and much of their supplies overland, presumably through Pennsylvania, with Ira and the men they had hired; they themselves traveled north to Lake Ontario, where they built boats. After portaging around Niagara Falls, they followed the shore of Lake Erie to the Cuyahoga River. The journey was arduous: they met ice at Niagara, a boat-wrecking storm in Lake Erie, and thievery that cost them critical supplies.

Reaching Cleveland at the mouth of the Cuyahoga River, they worked their boats upstream. As the water level of that often-shallow river allowed, they made their way south. It was spring, and rains probably provided water levels adequate to negotiate the many rocks and bars that characterize the bed of the serpentine river. They reached the entrance of Brandywine Creek, north of the present village of Peninsula, and there brought their goods ashore onto level, but marshy, ground.

Thence they proceeded overland through rain to their landholdings: Hudson in Range 10, Township 4; Tappan in Range 8, Township 3.

Hudson reached his new land on June 17, 1799. The trip had taken forty-eight days. There he met the overland party that brought cattle and much-needed supplies. He set about laying out a village on high land just southwest of the center of his holding and built a cabin. He and his men planted wheat and corn in a newly cleared field. A spring was tapped for water. Game was plentiful and provided meat. Hudson was well pleased with his new land. He and Ira returned to Goshen in October. Some of the men he had hired remained and spent the winter in Hudson's cabin.

Back in Connecticut, Hudson sold tracts of his holdings to a number of his Connecticut neighbors. In January 1800 Hudson, this time with his wife and six children, set out once again for the arduous journey westward. His party included other settlers and their families. Supplies and equipment were purchased. Along the way, boats were built for the water portion of the trip. On May 28 they reached the mouth of Brandywine Creek on the Cuyahoga River. Hudson set out alone on horseback to his cabin and the men he had left behind the preceding winter. Returning two days later, he found his company in misery, plagued by hordes of mosquitoes from the surrounding swamps. He led the group overland to their new homesteads. There they soon celebrated the Fourth of July with a communal feast.

The new town grew with the arrival of additional settlers. David Hudson and his fellow settlers in the newly founded community established a church shortly after their arrival. On June 5, 1800, they held their first worship service in a log cabin. In 1802 Hudson and twelve other residents of the new village established the Congregational Church of Hudson. In 1820 they erected a church on the east side of the public square of their young but growing town.

Hudson built a substantial frame house on the main road leading north. It was finished in 1806. The first frame building in Hudson and the most sizeable structure in the young town, it served not only as the Hudson residence but also as town hall and, when needed, a church meeting house. When travelers came to Hudson, it served as a guest house. The house stands today at 318 North Main Street in Hudson.

Hudson played a continuing role in the development of the community that bore his name. As the nineteenth century dawned, the residents of the Western Reserve found it increasingly difficult to attract clergy to serve their religious needs. With several Presbyterian presbyteries taking the lead, citizens began to organize themselves into groups advocating the establishment of a seminary in the Western Reserve. After much political wrangling, a site on land owned by David Hudson in the northern part of the village was chosen. Hudson donated the site, located on a ridge across the road from his frame house, and took the lead in raising funds to establish what became Western Reserve College.

In December 1825 the backers of the proposed institution approached the Ohio legislature with their request for a charter for a college that would include a theology department. Their petition was not well received, for there were many who argued that it was inappropriate to link a seminary with other educational programs. Of the eighteen theological schools in the United States at that time, only the one at Yale was affiliated with a broader educational institution. After much political maneuvering, the legislature granted a charter on February 7, 1826. As part of the political give and take, the founding of Kenyon College was also authorized in response to a petition from the Episcopal Church in Ohio, that act taking place on January 24. In the compromises leading to the charter given to Western Reserve College, reference to a theology department was dropped. In its place, permission was granted to establish schools for education in any discipline (including, but not specifically stated, theology), thus making Western Reserve College one of the first true universities in the United States.[12]

4

Connecticut

Born and raised in Wallingford, Connecticut, Turhand Kirtland had settled into a career as a carriage maker there. He was a veteran of the American Revolution and had witnessed the British conquest of New York City and subsequent ravaging of Connecticut towns. Kirtland had become a well-known and respected member of the community. On January 2, 1780, he married Mary Beach. They lived in Wallingford until the young woman died on November 24, 1782, less than two years after their wedding. What illness might have taken her is not known, but many infectious diseases were prevalent in that area at the time. Death in young adulthood was all too common.

After more than a decade as a widower, the then thirty-seven-year-old Turhand Kirtland married again on January 18, 1793. His second wife, twenty-year-old Mary Potter, always known as Polly, was the daughter of Wallingford's leading medical practitioner, Dr. Jared Potter. Her blue silk damask wedding gown is now preserved at the Mahoning Valley Historical Society in Youngstown, Ohio. Polly was known in Wallingford and later in Poland, where they settled in the Western Reserve, as a gracious and well-educated lady. She was also an accomplished cook.

The couple welcomed their firstborn child on November 10, 1793. Polly named him Jared Potter to honor her father. Five more children followed: Henry Turhand, born in 1795; Mary Beach, born in 1798; Henry, born in 1801; Billius, born in 1807; and George, born in 1808. The first four children were born in Wallingford; the last two after the Kirtlands had moved to Poland in the Western Reserve.

Turhand Kirtland was a subscriber to the original draft of land by the Connecticut Land Company, drawing with his partners property in several townships, including Burton, Poland, about 2,000 acres in Kirtland, and portions of Auburn and Mecca Townships. At forty-two years old, he became the general land agent for the Connecticut Land Company. Jared Potter Kirtland was four years old when his father accepted this appointment.

Upon accepting the charge of representing the Connecticut Land Company, Turhand Kirtland became responsible for overseeing the surveying and sale of property in the Western Reserve. This duty required his presence in the newly established Western Reserve. Starting in the spring of 1798 he traveled back and forth annually between Ohio and Connecticut.[1]

Turhand Kirtland moved his family to Poland in 1803. The Kirtlands journeyed overland on a primitive road across Pennsylvania and the Allegheny Mountains in two covered wagons. It took a full month to reach their new home in Poland. For Polly the journey must have been especially arduous, for she was pregnant and due to deliver at the end of the summer.

Jared Potter Kirtland, however, remained in Connecticut, where there were more educational opportunities for him.[2] The young Jared Potter lived in the home of his grandparents. Jared Potter and his wife, Sarah Forbes, were already caring for the children of their older daughter. Sarah Potter had married Billius Kirtland, Turhand's younger brother and a respected doctor. Both died within ten days of each other in the fall of 1805. The causes of their deaths are not known, but an epidemic infectious disease would seem likely for two deaths less than two weeks apart. Sarah and Billius Kirtland left four children, Eliza, Polly, George, and Sarah, ranging in age from ten to sixteen at the time of their parents' deaths. Thus, when Jared Kirtland stayed in Wallingford with his grandparents, their house was full of youthful activity.

Dr. Jared Potter was a physician with a substantial reputation for clinical excellence.[3] Born in East Haven, Connecticut, on September 25, 1742, Potter attended Yale College, graduating in 1760. He then studied medicine with two local physicians, a typical course of training for doctors at that time. In 1763 he began practicing medicine in New Haven. He moved to Wallingford in 1773.

Potter was commissioned in 1775 as a physician and surgeon in the "First Regiment of Inhabitants Inlisted [sic] and Assembled for the Special Defense and Safety" of the colony of Connecticut under the command of General David Wooster. He served in the northern campaign and took charge of a hospital in Montreal. Later he served at the Battle of White Plains. Ill with what was thought to be tuberculosis, he was discharged on April 15, 1776. Kirtland recovered and returned to Wallingford. He resumed his medical practice and purchased a fifty-acre farm a half mile south of the town center.[4]

Much esteemed for his clinical acumen, Potter trained a number of other physicians. He developed a nostrum containing camphor, ammonia, chalk, and charcoal. Known as Potter's Powder, it was used for decades to treat stomach ailments. From a modern medical viewpoint, this prescription was certainly harmless and may have benefitted many with heartburn or other manifestations of indigestion. Potter was respected by his peers, an esteemed member of the Medical Society of New Haven County, and a founder of the state medical society. He was the first secretary of the state society and later its vice president.

Potter was a liberal thinker. Some of his religious ideas were considered heretical by the more orthodox of his neighbors. An early biographer, Charles Henry Stanley Davis, wrote, "He was a speculating theologian, and his speculations were of an infidel character; and it is said that his pupils, whatever progress they made in medical studies, generally left Dr. Potter's office with minds tinged with skeptical notions."[5] In his adult life, Jared Potter Kirtland would embrace liberal ideas—opposing slavery, for example. So also would he possess a healthy skepticism of orthodoxy in the world of taxonomy, which led him to reclassify many Ohio species. The seeds of those ideas were probably sown during his youth in Wallingford.

Kirtland's grandmother, Sarah Potter, may have been less liberal than her husband. During the American Revolution she apparently had royalist sympathies. In November 1852 Kirtland wrote to Benjamin Lossing, the publisher of a book on the American Revolution. He recounted a time when his grandmother sheltered a royalist leader in her home. Governor William Franklin of New Jersey was a Tory general who had been captured and was being held as a prisoner.

> Gov. F. was billeted out upon the family of Capt. Johnson, an innkeeper in the town of Wallingford ... in 1776. The house of Johnson was much thronged ... [and] was otherwise rendered uncomfortable. My grandfather, Dr. Jared Potter ...

owned a large, commodious and well-furnished house contiguous to that of Johnson....

By the urgent request of Gov. Franklin ... the Governor transferred his residence to my grandfather's family.... His time was mostly spent in reading but he daily walked in the garden and, if possible, would take along with him on his excursions my aunt and my mother, the one eight years old, the other six.[6]

Dr. Jared Potter was in Canada at the time serving as a surgeon with revolutionary forces there.

In an 1852 letter to Sarah Kirtland, one of his cousins, Kirtland wrote further of his recollections of Franklin's stay in the Potter home.

I have been corresponding with [Benjamin] Lossing, editor and publisher of the Pictorial Revolution in regard to the place of confinement of Gov. Franklin, natural son of Benjamin Franklin. Do you recall he boarded some time with Grandmother Potter while Grandfather was in Canada at Chambles and St. Johns, that he occupied your north chamber? What do you know of the matter? Lossing in his work says in one place that Gov. F. was detained as a prisoner at East Windsor and in another in Windham, Ct. Marshall in his Diary kept at Philadelphia during the Revolution says the Tory Gov. Franklin of New Jersey was confined a prisoner at Hartford, Ct. Now to my certain knowledge he was billeted on Capt. Johnson, innkeeper in the Jared Lewis House. The house was thronged with company and Gov. Franklin was far from comfortable. One of his Tory families prevailed upon Grandmother to take him into her family. She was, I think, a little of a Royalist in her ways of thinking. The Governor took such notice of her two little daughters who were then mere school children, so at his departure, so confident was he of the triumph of the Crown, that he charged Grandmother P. to appeal to him for aid when the Colonists were suffering the penalties for rebellion. I think that he was probably changed from place to place as a matter of safety.[7]

Subsequently Kirtland evidently had some doubts about the veracity of remarks to his cousin. He found evidence to support his memory, however. On April 11, 1853, he wrote again to his cousin Sarah.

> On investigating the imprisonment of Gov. Franklin I have been surprised to find how soon facts are lost or perverted in history. The fact that he was detained in Wallingford in Grandmother Potter's family had escaped the knowledge of every member of our family except myself and I began to fear that imagination might have been at work in my mind, but recently I have obtained evidence to sustain my assertion that he was located for a time as a prisoner in Wallingford. Esq. Hondley informs me that "in American Archives, Vol. 5th for 1776 it is stated that Gov. F. Franklin resided in Wallingford early in July and was removed from thence to Middletown and soon thereafter exchanged."[8]

Kirtland must have been amused by this episode, for he knew his grandfather to be a liberal and an ardent supporter of the American Revolution. Had he been home, he would not willingly have welcomed Governor Franklin into his home.

At the dawning of the nineteenth century, Wallingford was a village with a few dwellings and a prominent church. It was established as a town by court order on land originally part of New Haven on May 12, 1670. It was a center of Puritanism. Among the original signers of the covenant embraced by the villagers was Samuel Potter, one of Jared Potter's forebears. Not until mid-century, following growth of the community, would industry arrive in the form of silver plating, pewter manufacturing, and the production of flatware for the tables of American homes. Wallingford's first newspaper began publication in 1844.[9]

The young Kirtland's early education was at a district school in Wallingford. Upon the departure of his parents, he was enrolled in academies for his secondary education. Initially, in 1807, he matriculated at an academy in Wallingford. One year later, he transferred to the Episcopal Academy in nearby Cheshire; he finished there in 1810.

The Cheshire academy was chartered in Wallingford in 1794 by the Episcopal Bishop in America with the intent of educating future Episcopal clergy. Construction of a building was begun two years later, with a cornerstone laid in place on April 28, 1796, and completion of the building later that year. The school continues to the present as a coeducational, independent, college-preparatory school.

During the first decade of its existence, the Episcopal Academy in Cheshire floundered. Its mission uncertain, it was reorganized on at least two occasions. In 1806, the year preceding Jared Kirtland's enrollment, the Reverend Tillotson Bronson became the school's headmaster. Bronson graduated from Yale in 1786 and was ordained as an Episcopal deacon the following year.[10] He served as rector in several New England churches before assuming the post at Cheshire. Under his direction the school emphasized the classics, and students were allowed to practice the religion of their family's choice. Kirtland's library contained a copy of an *Episcopal Book of Common Prayer*. It is inscribed as belonging to him with a date of January 1, 1810. At that time he was in his last year as a student at the Cheshire Academy. Perhaps he acquired it as a gift from Bronson.

Kirtland excelled as a student, earning honors in mathematics, Greek, and Latin.[11] For a time he was a private pupil of Bronson's and lived with the Bronson family. A love of classics remained with Kirtland throughout his life. It was his practice to reread both the *Æneid* and the *Iliad* every year or two, and he enjoyed reading them in the original Greek and Latin. Neither work was included in the volumes donated to Western Reserve University by Kirtland's granddaughter. He surely must have had them; perhaps they were kept by one of his heirs.

As a young lad, Jared Kirtland had developed a close relationship with his grandfather, a relationship cemented by a mutual love of nature. Potter introduced all of his grandchildren to the natural world. He was especially attentive to Jared, for the boy was bright and took to the teachings of his grandfather with enthusiasm. From the older man, he learned to identify the birds and animals prevalent in the area. Potter introduced his grandson to botany, using his gardens and orchard as practical laboratories. Young Kirtland selectively cultivated flowers to produce desirable blooms. He learned the art of grafting to obtain desirable fruits and of cross pollinating to develop new varieties. Later in life he would employ these skills in his own orchards. Potter had bee-

hives, and Kirtland made observations of their behavior and their ene-
mies. Moreover, with his grandfather's guidance, he learned to keep
careful records of his observations.

Carl von Linné was an eighteenth-century Swedish physician who
loved flowers and planted gardens just as Potter did nearly a century
later. The Swedish doctor decided to classify the plants he studied. La-
tinizing his name to Carolus Linnæus, he published a tract entitled *Sys-
tema Naturae* in 1735. In this work, he classified all life forms in a
schema, the basic elements of which remain in use today. This system
assigned categories in a rank order, beginning with separation into animal and plant kingdoms and continuing to final genus and species des-
ignations. While other parts of Linnæus' schema have been modified
with the passage of time, the binomial nomenclature he established for
the flowers in his garden persists today. For plants and trees, Linnæus
used their reproductive systems—flowers and seeds—as the basis for
genus and species assignments. Thus, all trees that produce acorns are
oaks. Full-sized dogwood trees and ground-hovering bunchberry wild-
flowers are members of the same genus, as the identical appearances of
their flowers dictate. As a youth and with his mentor-grandfather's guidance, Jared Kirtland studied Linnæan botanical classification and became
familiar with its application.

Looking back on his boyhood years, Kirtland reflected that "he
rarely took part in the plays and amusements of the youngsters of his
age. He knew nothing of skating, wrestling, ball-playing, or games of
chance. Whether this was from a natural disposition or the effects of
habit and his grandfather's influence is not known."[12]

In the spring of 1810, Jared Kirtland received word that his father was
ill in Poland, perhaps seriously so. Taking leave from school, the six-
teen-year-old youth set out on horseback in May to make the journey
to the Western Reserve.[13] He was accompanied by Joshua Stow from
nearby Middletown, Connecticut. Traveling up the Mohawk River from
Albany, Kirtland encountered a canal where he observed, for the first
time, the operation of locks. At Utica the pair turned north, "called by
business" along the Black River for some thirty miles to reach Lowville.
There the young Kirtland observed limestone rocks bearing fossil shells

and imprints of organic materials, the origins of which he speculated upon. He spent time trout fishing in a small stream; the "creek was literally crowded with schools of that species. Fine specimens could be taken as fast as the hook could be baited and thrown into the water." In Lowville, they were joined by Alfred Kelley, who was traveling to Cleveland. Kelley would become a leading citizen of Northeast Ohio and the first elected mayor of Cleveland.

The travelers reached Buffalo on Lake Erie, then a village of "a few log houses and still fewer framed buildings." There Kirtland met Native Americans for the first time. The people he encountered were far from romantic, noble, Rousseauean figures and also far from savage, threatening warriors. Alcohol had reached these exploited people. "Red Jacket and many of his people might be seen by noon every day, taking a nap in a state of beastly drunkenness."

Buffalo was crowded with travelers waiting for favorable winds. Food was in short supply.

> Every bed and room were full, and provisions were scarce.
> Had not an abundant supply of fresh fish been furnished from
> the Lake, great inconvenience would have been experienced.
> As it was, Fish for breakfast, Fish for dinner, and Fish for
> supper was the invariable bill of fare. The cooks however
> manifested some ingenuity in varying their dishes through
> broiling, boiling, frying and chowder.[14]

While spending several days in Buffalo, Kirtland studied Great Lakes fish that local fishermen showed him. Ever the naturalist, he carefully described them and drew them. He also dissected them. Kirtland's interest in fish would continue throughout his life, and he found the waters of Lake Erie of great interest. Shallowest of the Great Lakes, Lake Erie continues to have more abundant and diverse fish populations than other freshwater environments.

Continuing along the lake, Kirtland and his companions found that the road, which had been laid out on high ground away from the shore, was deep in mud and clogged with fallen trees and stumps. They persevered, crossing Pennsylvania where it abuts Lake Erie to reach Painesville. Kirtland's traveling companions continued west to Cleveland, while he journeyed onward in the company of General Simon Perkins, who had reached the Western Reserve early, prospered, and accumulated considerable wealth. The two traveled to Warren and then on to Youngstown, where they arrived on June 11, 1810. They spent the night with a Dr. Dutton, who had studied medicine in Connecticut with Dr. Jared Potter. The next day Jared Potter Kirtland arrived in Poland.

> No bridges then spanned the Mahoning [River]. We passed over at Power's ford, the water high and muddy from recent rains; but the doctor [Dutton] pointed out a rock in the river, with its top barely visible above the water, which, he said, was an index that when the top appeared it was safe to ford the stream.[15]

Poland was at that time, in Kirtland's words, "a sparsely settled village of one street, the houses mostly log structures, a few frame buildings excepted; of the latter character was the dwelling house and store of Colonel Rayen."[16] However, he noted, it had "an air of activity and thriftiness, not observable at that time in all of the new settlements."[17] These descriptions date to Kirtland's later years and probably are not completely accurate. At the time of Kirtland's trip, Rayen was not yet a colonel, and his store was located at Spring Common in Youngstown.

When Kirtland arrived in Poland, he found that his father was not seriously ill. Turhand Kirtland had a swollen lymph gland in his neck, for which a local practitioner had given an ominous prognosis with the assumption that it was due to cancer or perhaps tuberculosis. However, that proved not to be the case, and he recovered.

Turhand Kirtland had already planted gardens and started an apiary, to which Jared Potter Kirtland brought the interest and experience he had acquired at his grandfather's home in Wallingford. Soon the younger Kirtland found himself teaching in the district school. In a letter written in 1874, he reminisced on this experience.

> In the following week I took charge of the district school in the village of Poland, consisting of sixty scholars, which I taught till late in September in a log house on the public square. Reading, writing, spelling, arithmetic and geography were the branches to be taught.[18]

Kirtland further commented on his students and his role as their teacher.

> The population furnishing the scholars was made up of various nationalities, and their pursuits were equally multifarious. Uniformity in only one matter prevailed, an opposition to everything like system, order and discipline; and in the schoolroom the children knew nothing of subordination. By perseverance in the exercise of patience and kindness on the part of the teacher, the respect and obedience of the pupils were secured, and their ambition awakened to learn the ordinary branches taught and they also improved in manners and good breeding.[19]

Dr. Jared Potter died suddenly in Wallingford, Connecticut, on July 8, 1810, the victim of an infection in his mouth resulting from a wound caused by a bit of rye grass that he had picked in his field.[20] When word of his death reached Kirtland in Poland, he set out to return to Wallingford. He bade adieu to his Ohio friends, and in company with Joshua Atwater commenced his return journey on horseback to Connecticut by way of Pittsburgh and over the Allegheny Mountains. It was not an easy journey. The roads were steep, rough, rocky, and frequently wet. Progress across the mountainous terrain proceeded at a snail's pace.

Potter had told his grandson that he hoped he would study medicine in Edinburgh, Scotland, which at the time was regarded as the pinnacle of medical education available in English. He left much of his estate to Kirtland, including his library of medical books. There were sufficient funds available for the young man to go to Edinburgh and pursue his medical education. However, the looming hostilities of the War of 1812 precluded this plan. Instead, Kirtland turned to Yale University and the recently chartered Yale School of Medicine.

As early as 1640, clergymen in the colony of Connecticut had tried to establish education for the youth of New Haven. Those early efforts were not sustained, however. Yale University was founded in Saybrook, Connecticut, in 1701. Its charter stated that the new school was established so that, "Youth may be instructed in the Arts and Sciences [and] through the blessing of Almighty God may be fitted for Publick [sic] employment both in Church and Civil State." At that time, preparation for religious ministry was generally accepted as the primary goal of higher education. Yale's charter provided a broader mandate. A true university was to be established. Yale acquired its name in 1718 when Elihu Yale, a merchant born in Wrexham, Wales, gave the university the proceeds from the sale of nine bales of hay, his library of 417 books, and a portrait of King George I.

An era of university-based medical education was slowly dawning in North America at that time. Most medical education, in Europe as well as in America, was rooted in apprenticeships with practicing physicians. These were often supplemented by lectures offered by practicing physicians, who charged their students attendance fees. Clinical experience was slow to enter the curricula of the new university-based medical schools, as university hospitals were uncommon. Thus, students sought and needed apprenticeships with established practitioners.

The Yale School of Medicine was the first post-baccalaureate school established by the university. Chartered in 1810, it was the sixth university-affiliated medical school established in America. Two faculty members, Nathan Smith and Benjamin Silliman, received their first students in 1812, Jared Potter Kirtland among them. Indeed, he was the first student to sign the matriculating book.[21] Smith was a highly respected physician and surgeon, well-suited to teach the clinical aspects of medicine. He had studied at Harvard with the eminent John Warren. His 1790 graduation thesis was titled *The Circulation of the Blood*. He then studied further in Edinburgh. Prior to joining the new faculty at Yale, Smith held teaching posts at Dartmouth and Bowdoin Colleges.[22]

Silliman was a remarkable man.[23] A Phi Beta Kappa graduate of Yale, he had joined the faculty as a professor to teach natural philosophy and chemistry. His knowledge also extended to geology and botany. He founded the *American Journal of Science and Arts*, the country's first scientific journal. Silliman quickly gained a reputation as an excellent lecturer and preceptor. With the opening of the School of Medicine, he was appointed professor of chemistry and pharmacy. At that time, pharmaceutical interventions were more often the products of botany than of chemistry. That such a man was named as one of the school's founding professors indicated a break from the empiric, clinical-tutor-based medical curriculum most common in the era. The best and most relevant science of the time was to be taught.

Shortly after his return to Connecticut, Kirtland started studying clinical medicine in Wallingford as an apprentice to Dr. John Andrews, a former pupil of Jared Potter's. Andrews had a large practice and was well-read in medicine. In 1812 Kirtland moved to Hartford to begin studying with Dr. Sylvester Wells. Not long thereafter he began private studies with the aforementioned Smith and Dr. Eli Ives, a distinguished physician who had joined the Yale faculty. He would continue to study with both after he enrolled in Yale in the autumn of 1812. For two years, Kirtland studied at Yale. The course of medical lectures offered by Smith and the other faculty members was concluded within a year. For the following year, Kirtland and some of his fellow students continued their studies, not only in tutorials offered by Smith and Silliman but also in a course in botany from Ives and an additional course in mineralogy with Silliman. He also supplemented his Yale education with additional clinical preceptorships with his original mentors, Drs. John Andrews and Sylvester Wells.

In early 1814, Kirtland briefly dropped his study of medicine. John S. Newberry, Kirtland's former student, fellow naturalist, and eulogist, implies that Kirtland did so for reasons of health.[24] It is also possible that he was having doubts about his career path. Regardless, there was no more than a few months' pause in his pursuit of a medical education. Illness among his neighbors and friends led him to employ his clinical skills, and the experience gave him confidence and encouragement to resume his studies. Soon thereafter Kirtland entered the University of Pennsylvania School of Medicine in Philadelphia. Founded in 1765, it was the first medical school in North America. Its faculty included Benjamin Rush, arguably the most prominent doctor in the country at that time. Rush was a professor of both medical practice and chemistry. He wrote the first American textbook of chemistry. Rush is also remembered for his political activity. He was a signer of the Declaration of Independence. Kirtland would have heard his lectures.

At the University of Pennsylvania, Kirtland wrote a thesis titled "Our Indigenous Vegetable Materia Medica" under the preceptorship of Botany Professor Benjamin S. Barton. He also studied under Professors Wistar, Physic Dorsey, Chapman, and James.[25]

Kirtland returned to Yale and received his MD degree from the school in 1815. His thesis, required for graduation, was titled "The Emetics Furnished by Our Indigenous Vegetation." Within five years Kirtland had received as comprehensive and excellent a medical education as could be found anywhere in North America. However, two books that Kirtland purchased on his way back to Yale attest to his continued love of gardening and nature: *McMahon's Gardeners Calendar* and *Forsyth on Fruit Trees*. Educated in medicine, he nonetheless retained the horticultural interests instilled in him by his grandfather.

While studying at Yale, Kirtland pursued his interests in natural history informally as well as in classes. He compiled a catalog of plants native to the New Haven region. As he had been taught by his grandfather, he kept a careful and complete record of his observations. He titled his handwritten journal *A Collection of Genera of Plants found in the Vicinity of New Haven 1814*. It contains hundreds of careful botanical descriptions. It is not clear whether the descriptions are Kirtland's or were simply copied from a field manual that he might have carried with him. In any case, they reveal a love of nature, a scholarly mind, and an understanding of Linnaean classification.

Botany was an important field of knowledge for physicians of that time, for most of the medications available were herbal. Botany had been included in Kirtland's studies with Silliman and Ives as well as in his curriculum in Philadelphia. Thanks to the tutoring he received from his grandfather, Kirtland's understanding of the biological world was broader than just herbal pharmaceutics.

At about the time Kirtland received his medical degree from Yale, Professor Silliman, whom Kirtland revered as one of his best teachers, issued a prospectus for the publication of the *American Journal of Science and Arts*. Kirtland was among the original subscribers. It was in this journal that Kirtland would later publish his landmark paper on the classification of freshwater mussels. He annually renewed his subscription throughout the remainder of his life.

In 1815, two months after completing his medical studies, Kirtland married Caroline Atwater, the daughter of Joshua Atwater, a prosperous merchant. The Atwater family traced its lineage back to the founding of Wallingford. John Atwater, Caroline's great-grandfather, was one of the village's original settlers.

The marriage was a happy one. Three children followed: Mary Elizabeth in 1816, Jared in 1818, and Caroline in 1821. Kirtland continued his interests in natural history—they would endure throughout his life—and he took on responsibility for the orchards and gardens that his grandfather had left to Kirtland's grandmother.

The young doctor began practice in Wallingford. Kirtland's father urged him to move to Poland, where there were no doctors. In 1818 Kirtland traveled to the Western Reserve to make arrangements to open a practice there. He made the arduous trip by stagecoach as far as Pittsburgh. Unable to find transportation into Ohio, he set out on foot down the right bank of the Ohio River.

Upon his return to Wallingford, he found that he had been elected a probate judge, possibly nominated by Caroline, who preferred to remain in Connecticut. Clearly, Jared Potter Kirtland was a respected young man in his community. Honored by the trust of his neighbors, he accepted the position and served the one-year term, putting aside thoughts of Poland.

Ten miles east of Wallingford in Durham, Connecticut, there was great need for a physician. A town meeting in that community passed a resolution inviting Kirtland to open a practice there. The Kirtlands moved to Durham. Citizens of that town welcomed him and assured him his practice would prosper there. He purchased a house from Heth F. Camp.

Kirtland thrived in Durham. He wrote of his life there:

> In that town at this period, an intelligent, kind and social set of manners prevailed through the whole population; the imprint of one or more past generations. More wealth, splendor and show, as well as vice, could be found in other Connecticut towns; but here were order, civility, and the very essence of good breeding—the art of making every one comfortable and happy....
>
> The young and middle-aged formed and made one social circle. Its meetings were frequent, and into it little that was frivolous found its way, and less that was malevolent and scandalizing. Its influence soon become manifest in my own manners and expressions. Hitherto retired, cold, melancholic, I became cheerful and social, with an entire change of deportment.[26]

Kirtland found that the religious skepticism instilled in him by his grandfather faded while he was in Durham. In the same letter quoted above he wrote:

> The Rev. David Smith's ... example and precepts corrected my skeptical views of religion, which I had formed early in life, and through life confirmed me in the truth of the Christian religion.

It is of interest that Smith's records for the Christian Church in Durham, which list all of the congregation's members and all of the baptisms he performed, do not mention either Kirtland or his wife.[27] A large family Bible in nearly pristine condition was found in Kirtland's Rockport home when it was sold many years after his death. It contains notations of his marriage to Caroline Atwater and the births of their three children, but they are not in his handwriting. Thereafter there are no further entries. Presumably this Bible was brought into the home by his wife and ignored by him after her death.

Kirtland's penciled marginal notes in his copy of Fowler's 1866 history of Connecticut provide further insights into his life in Durham.[28] He continued his interests in natural history. He described Thomas Lyman as "the best bird man in Durham." Commenting on his medical practice, he noted that he attended Simeon Parsons in his last illness and that he was the family physician of Dan Parmalee and his family.

In 1820 an epidemic of a disease characterized by fever erupted in Durham and neighboring regions of Connecticut. In Kirtland's letter cited above, he called it "malignant typhus fever." The germ that causes typhus is a disease carried by lice. Typhus is an ancient disease that has occurred in major epidemics. It carries about a 20 percent mortality rate in adults. In children, the disease is usually mild. (Thus, it would be a logical explanation for the earlier deaths of Billius Kirtland and his wife, with their children spared.) Others referred to the epidemic as "sinking typhoid fever."

In fact, typhus and typhoid were often confused by physicians at that time and the terminology of these two diseases was often interchanged. Water-borne typhoid it could have been, for sanitary water and sewage systems had yet to arrive. Not until 1857 did William Budd establish the relation of typhoid to sewage in Tawnton, Devonshire, England.

Kirtland's lecture notes from his later years as a medical school professor make it clear that he knew of both typhus and typhoid, but neither those notes nor available contemporaneous accounts allow an accurate discrimination between the two illnesses that plagued much of Connecticut at the time.[29] Whatever this disease might have been, it struck hard at the young Kirtland family. One-year-old Caroline died in 1822. Death struck her mother on September 18, 1823.

Kirtland was devastated by the deaths of his daughter and wife. Within a year he had shut the door on his Connecticut life and moved to Poland. Despondent, he decided to give up medicine and devote his life to agriculture in the new land of the Western Reserve.

5

Poland

When Jared Potter Kirtland joined his parents in the Western Reserve in 1823, Poland was the fastest-growing community in the area. It was home to a small community of migrants from Connecticut, many of them part of the extended Kirtland family. Many migrants from western Pennsylvania of German and Northern Irish stock had also settled in Poland.

Kirtland intended to leave medicine behind when he moved from Connecticut to his father's house at the southeast corner of the Western Reserve. He disposed of his property and most of his possessions other than his books, which he shipped to Ohio. He left his two surviving children with relatives; they would join him later.

Kirtland planned to devote his life to horticulture, which he loved. He had developed an orchard in Durham, and he shipped stocks of fruit and ornamental trees and shrubbery to Ohio ahead of his arrival. He purchased additional horticultural items from Michael Floy, who had an extensive nursery at that time on Broadway in New York City.[1]

Kirtland wanted to be a farmer. His father gave him 243 acres in Boardman Township, just west of Poland, and built a house for him, which was completed in 1826. Within a year Kirtland was working in his brothers' orchard and had established his own orchard and a greenhouse as well. He used the grafting and pollination skills he had learned from his grandfather to develop new varieties of fruit.[2] His younger brothers—Henry, already an accomplished gardener and orchardist, and Billius—joined him in this enterprise. Henry had opened a store in 1825, and he regularly traveled east to obtain merchandise. Kirtland pored over catalogues and arranged for his brother to bring back cuttings and seedlings of more than one hundred varieties of cherries, peaches, pears, and apples, in addition to many other plants from New England and New York. From these he developed new varieties. The Kirtland nursery would eventually be regarded as one of the most outstanding facilities of its kind in Ohio. A 1904 history of Ohio agriculture extolled his success and reputation at his orchard and nursery.

> In 1824 Professor J. P. Kirtland and his brother established a nursery at Poland, which was then located in Trumbull county. They brought from New England over one hundred of the best varieties of apples, cherries, peaches, pears, etc.; and a year or two later they brought over one hundred varieties from New Jersey and others were secured from New York. Dr. Kirtland, by his system of hybridization, produced over thirty varieties of cherries.[3]

Kirtland occasionally helped in Henry's store. For the most part, however, he was busy with his farm, greenhouse, and nursery. He began to expand his interests in natural history from their Connecticut origins. Perhaps thanks to his prosperous father, he was comfortable financially. He owned one of only five carriages in Poland.

There was no doctor in Poland, so Kirtland soon found himself once again caring for the sick. Typhoid fever—or an illness thought to be typhoid—was common in the area at that time. It had taken the lives of two of the four doctors practicing in the area. On arrival in Poland Kirtland spent the night in his father's house. Early the following morning he was called five miles away to care for a man dying of typhoid pneumonia.

In 1824 Kirtland opened a pharmacy store in the center of the town. Not much is known of it. One can suppose that he might have dispensed his grandfather's remedy, Potter's Powders. By 1830 Kirtland was widely recognized as one of the most skilled physicians in the Western Reserve.

In 1829, Kirtland traveled to Columbus to begin a term in the state legislature. He needed a doctor to fill in for him when he had to attend legislative sessions. He recruited a young physician, Eli Mygatt, to join him in his practice.[4]

Born in 1807 in Canfield, less than ten miles west of Poland, My-gatt had attended West Point, where he had befriended his classmate Jefferson Davis. He left West Point after one year to become a seaman. Unhappy with seafaring, he returned to Canfield and began studying medicine with a Dr. Fowler. He attended medical lectures at the Fairfield Medical College in central New York along the usual route from New England to the Western Reserve. There he studied with John Delamater, who would later become one of the founders of the Medical Department of Western Reserve College (now the School of Medicine of Case Western Reserve University).

Mygatt joined Kirtland in Poland on a Sunday; Kirtland left for Columbus the next day. For a period of time, Mygatt may also have lived in the Kirtland home. In 1831 he married Kirtland's cousin, Lois, daughter of Turhand Kirtland's brother Jared, and presumably left the Kirtland household. He continued to practice in Poland. He died in 1885.

Reflecting years later on his practice with Mygatt, Kirtland described an incident of surgery under improvised circumstances.

In Surgery, [we] did an extensive practice, and gained much credit by performing a number of important operations. Medical and surgical paraphernalia were not easily obtained in those days in the back woods.... On one occasion [we] were called into another town to see a woman whose hip was dislocated, and two surgeons who had vainly attempted to replace the bone, pronounced it irreducible. [We] thought otherwise. With the aid of a cabinet maker and blacksmith, [we] manufactured an ingenious set of blocks and tackles, made everything ready for their application, immersed the patient in a hot bath, opened a vein in each arm and administered emetic tartar till faintness and relaxation ensued. She was promptly placed on the table, extension made, and the dislocation reduced the ninth day after the accident.[5]

Kirtland was called to testify in a malpractice suit of a Dr. Hawley, who was sued after a surgical procedure that he and other physicians thought had been well-performed.

A woman was thrown from a horse; a compound dislocation of the ankle joint produced, the lower end of the fibula driven into the ground, bruised and abraded by its periosteum, and the cavity filled with dirt. A council of doctors proposed amputation, as all military surgeons would have done. She and friends objected. The doctor then proceeded to cleanse the wound of all cause of irritation, took off the tip of the abraded fibula, reduced the dislocation and ultimately the wound healed successfully; of course ankylosis of the joint followed. The patient not only refused to pay the doctors's bill, but commenced a suit for heavy damages on the charge of malpractice.

The judge charged [sic] decidedly in favor of the defense, yet the jury to the astonishment of all intelligent persons, brought in a verdict of four thousand dollars damages for the plaintiff.[6]

As a result of this experience, Kirtland excluded surgery from his practice. In his words, he "positively refused to give advice, express and opinion, or in any manner commit himself by practicing in any surgical case."[7]

Once he had recovered from the depression that followed the deaths of his daughter and wife, Kirtland remarried. Trumbull County, Ohio, court records indicate that Jared T. [sic] Kirtland married Hannah Fitch Toucey of Warren on March 25, 1824.[8] There is little additional information about her that can be reliably confirmed. An 1890 posthumous tribute to Kirtland stated erroneously that this marriage took place in 1825 and that the bride was Hannah Fitch Toucey of Newtown, Connecticut.[9] The Toucey family was an old Puritan family with its members present in many Connecticut towns. The vital records of Newtown make no mention of Hannah Toucey's birth nor of a marriage that could have been of her parents.[10] Hannah Fitch Toucey's Fitch antecedents can also be inferred, but not documented. She was reported in a local newspaper account to have been a niece of Zalmon Fitch, who settled in Warren northwest of Poland.[11] Early members of the Fitch family were founders of Norwalk, Connecticut.

Not only is it difficult to ascertain Hannah Toucey Kirtland's antecedents, but it is remarkable how little documentation of her life as

Kirtland's wife exists. There are occasional references to her in accounts of Rockport civic functions, and Kirtland refers to her health in his letters. However, the memoir he dictated late in his life, which comprises twenty-eight single-spaced pages in the typed transcript, makes no mention of her.

Hannah Kirtland now rests in Lake View Cemetery in Cleveland, Ohio. Her tombstone gives her name as Hannah F. T. Kirtland; her name in the cemetery's records is Hannah F. Kirtland. Her date of death is given on the marker as December 23, 1857, and she is stated to have been "ag'd 58 y'rs." Thus, she was probably born in or about 1799. It should be noted, however, that this stone was commissioned when her son-in-law, Charles Pease, purchased a plot and moved all of his deceased relatives from other cemeteries to the site in 1883, a quarter century after her death.[12] He would have relied on his memory and that of his wife, Kirtland's daughter, in commissioning the marker. The 1830 census lists two free white females in Kirtland's household. One, age 15 to 19, would have been his daughter, Mary Elizabeth, actually age fourteen. The other was listed as age 40 to 49. Ten years later, in the 1840 census, the Kirtland household includes a free white female age 50 to 59. These census records almost certainly refer to Hannah. If her age at death was close to that on her tombstone, then she was probably in her early or midthirties in 1830 and early or midforties in 1840.

The house that Turhand Kirtland built for his son in Poland in 1826 was moved from its original site near the center of town and restored in 1976. It still stands and is occupied today. The first floor contained a parlor and kitchen, both reasonably large, and a small room that was probably Kirtland's office or study.

By the end of the third decade of the nineteenth century, Jared Potter Kirtland—called "Potter" by his friends and family—had become a leading figure in the Western Reserve. Elected to the state legislature by the citizens of what was then Trumbull County, he served three two-year terms, the first beginning December 7, 1829, the subsequent ones in December 1831 and 1834.[13] The Ohio and Erie Canal was functioning smoothly in the pre-railroad era and was of great economic importance to the Western Reserve. A spur—designated the Pennsylvania and Ohio

Canal—linking the Ohio and Erie Canal at Akron with Pennsylvania's canal system had been proposed. The Ohio proposal was vigorously opposed by the Sandy and Beaver Canal Company of Pennsylvania. Legislator Kirtland was influential in obtaining passage of the supporting legislation for that venture and for ensuring that it would be built by Ohioans. It opened in 1840.

In the legislature Kirtland took interest in laws proposed to establish a state penitentiary system. He chaired a committee on the penitentiary. Prisons at the time were operated by private contractors who held inmates in small cells and exploited their labor. A visit to a prison in Columbus was a disturbing eye-opener. It led Kirtland to take an active role in prison reform.

> [He] drew up a report detailing the failure of the old prison in every point of view, recommending its abandonment and the erection of new buildings in a different locality. It also embraced [an] improved system of discipline....
>
> . The bill first came up in the House and met with strong opposition from various quarters. It would endanger a flourishing commerce carried on through the medium of the corrupt guards, by which ... articles manufactured within the walls and stolen by the convicts were exchanged for whiskey and tobacco with certain grocer and liquor dealers in Columbus.[14]

Under Kirtland's leadership, Ohio established a system of state-operated prisons that emphasized discipline and the humane treatment of prisoners.

Tragedy struck once again when Kirtland's son, Jared Jr., died on August 15, 1829, at age eleven. The circumstances of his death are not known. Kirtland's daughter, Mary Elizabeth, remained as his only child; at age sixteen she married twenty-one-year-old Charles Pease (a nephew of surveyor Seth Pease) in 1832.

Hannah Fitch Toucey Kirtland bore no children. The Kirtland home frequently echoed with children's voices, however. Kirtland's sister Mary Beach Kirtland and her husband, Richard Hall, both died at early ages, and their two daughters, Mary and Lucy, became part of the household. Other children followed. Kirtland's sister Nancy also died at a young age, and her two sons, Henry and Edwin Morse, came under the wing of Potter and Hannah. When Kirtland moved to Cleveland, the Morse boys would take over the Poland nursery. Nephew Alfred, son of Billius, was frequently present in the house. Potter and Hannah also took in an orphaned boy, but details of this matter are not known. Kirtland taught all of these youngsters about the joys he felt in the natural world. Four dogs joined the household and followed Kirtland as he walked his land.

Among the children in the Kirtland home was his first grandchild, the son of Mary Elizabeth and Charles Pease. Born on July 18, 1834, he was named Jared Potter Kirtland Pease. He was born with congenital valvular heart disease and thus doomed to a short life. He died on December 17, 1836. Kirtland was devastated. He wrote to his friend, Samuel Hildreth.

> On arriving home from Columbus I found my little grandson and namesake in the last stage of cyanotic suffocation in which he continued in the utmost agony for 36 hours. His death has again blasted my expectations and surrounded me with that melancholy void which was created by the loss of my only son a few years hence (Aug 15, 1829). This little grandson had been adopted into my family and had already done much towards supplying the place of my son.[15]

It is unknown whether Kirtland maintained the religious beliefs he had come to hold in Wallingford. He probably did not attend religious services in the Western Reserve, despite his staunchly Episcopalian father's presence. Bound with other miscellaneous papers in Kirtland's library were copies of the proceedings of annual conventions of the Episcopal Church of Ohio in 1824, 1825, and 1827. It is unlikely that Kirtland attended these meetings. However, his parents and his wife, Hannah, might well have. The lists of lay delegates included in these proceedings do not mention any of Kirtland's family members, however. A later letter to Hildreth indicates that he might attend such an event in Cincinnati in 1835; it is not known whether he did so.

Kirtland made his house a station on the Underground Railroad. At one time he calmly entertained bounty hunters who were searching for two runaway slaves. Kirtland fed them in his kitchen and then toured them through his farm and outbuildings to assure them that the slaves were not on his property. Throughout this, the two escapees were hiding in the parlor, which Kirtland managed not to show the bounty hunters. Learning that a runaway slave named Kitty was in Ashtabula on the shore of Lake Erie, Kirtland traveled to that community and paid the bounty for her so that she could become a free woman. She became part of his household and was found there by the 1830 census. She was said to be age 20 to 29 at that time.

In 1837 Daniel Drake recruited Kirtland to the professorship of the theory and practice of physic—the then-common designation for professorships in what is now called internal medicine—at his newly founded Ohio College of Medicine in Cincinnati. Kirtland later described the circumstances surrounding this recruitment.

> The intimate acquaintance formed on [the] occasion [of the malpractice trial presided over by] Judge Wright, produced ulterior results. In the autumn of 1835 ... without previous intimation or a dream of such an occurrence, [I] received from the Board of Trustees of the Medical College of Ohio an appointment to the Professorship of Theory and Practice of Medicine, and at the same time a letter from Judge Wright, a member of that Board, stating that the appointment was made by his nomination, and urging [me] to accept.[16]

Taking up a professorship was not an activity to which Kirtland aspired, although his subsequent success as a professor makes it clear he was well-suited to this role. In fact, it was the potential income that attracted him to Cincinnati. Economic downturns were frequent in the mid-nineteenth century, and Kirtland suffered financially. Additionally, he found himself facing the costs of caring for his daughter, who was so depressed by the loss of her son that she required nursing care. In February 1837 Kirtland wrote from Poland to Samuel Hildreth about his new professorship.

> You will probably be somewhat surprised to learn that I have received a notice of an appointment to the Professorship of the Theory and Practice of Med. In the Ohio Med. College at

Cincinnati & that I have accepted of the trust.
The situation of my finances compelled me to take this
step. I am busily engaged in preparing my lectures.[17]

In addition to his lectures, Kirtland was required to conduct clinics and make rounds at the Cincinnati Hospital, for which he was the responsible physician during the academic term.

Daniel Drake was one of the more improbable figures in the history of midwestern medicine.[18] His father, Isaac Drake, an impoverished New Jersey farmer, was an early settler near what is today Lexington, Kentucky. Daniel received scant formal education. At age fifteen, his father apprenticed him to Dr. William Goforth in Cincinnati. Drake's father had met Goforth in Kentucky, where he was the only physician serving the few pioneers there. Goforth, who had little formal medical education, later moved to Cincinnati, and the teenaged Drake left his Kentucky home to join him there for his apprenticeship.

Drake lived with the Goforth family, and before many months had passed he was making rounds with the doctor and assuming responsibility for the care of some of his patients. In 1805, Goforth issued Drake a medical diploma. Shortly thereafter, Goforth left Cincinnati for New Orleans, and Drake took over his practice. Despite the lack of more formal credentials, Drake enjoyed a reputation as a skilled physician. He read medical texts as he could obtain them. He planned to study medicine at the University of Pennsylvania, but initially found it beyond his financial means. Ten years later, in 1815, he finally found the resources to study in Philadelphia, where he eventually received a degree from the University of Pennsylvania.

The first medical school beyond the Appalachian Mountains opened in Kentucky at Transylvania University in Lexington in 1815. The founders of the new school offered Drake a professorship, which he accepted with alacrity. "I am a professor, ... [a] really and bona fide appointed ... professor, ... unquestionably a professor," he wrote to a friend.[19] He was a popular lecturer at the new medical school, where he spent the winter months of the medical school term. He returned to Cincinnati the following summer, when school was not in session, and soon began organizing a new medical school in that city. He resigned his position at Transylvania, having served there only one term. His efforts to establish a medical school in Cincinnati were successful; the

Medical College of Ohio in that city was chartered in 1819. It opened the following November and soon become the most respected medical school in the American West.

Diplomacy among his medical colleagues was never one of Drake's virtues, and after just five years his fellow Cincinnati faculty members, most of whom he had personally recruited, voted to dismiss him. Transylvania welcomed him back. His repeat tenure in Lexington was short-lived, and soon he returned to Cincinnati, where he attempted to organize another medical school, the medical department of Cincinnati College, again called the Medical College of Ohio. After an auspicious start, this venture collapsed after four years when Drake's faculty resigned en masse. Drake moved to Louisville, Kentucky, where he tried without success once again to organize a medical school.

Given the tumultuous nature of Drake's ventures into medical education, it is not surprising that Jared Potter Kirtland was readily recruited to join a medical school in Willoughby in 1842. In fact, it is surprising that he continued his affiliation with the Medical College of Ohio in Cincinnati as long as he did.

After assuming his new professorship at Willoughby, Kirtland took up residence in Cleveland. The city was thriving. Factories and mills had arrived. A fire department had been organized, as had a local Temperance Society. There were two newspapers. Canal boats transferred their cargo to schooners plying Lake Erie; indeed this water-borne traffic was the stimulus for much of Cleveland's growth. The opening of the Erie Canal and the Ohio and Erie Canal had aided Cleveland's prosperity and growth. Residential and suburban neighborhoods developed on the western side of the Cuyahoga River. Warehouses were built to serve the growing river and Lake Erie shipping industry. Many commercial enterprises developed. The population grew rapidly. The 1850 census counted 17,034 residents; that of 1860 counted 43,838. It was in this thriving city, a city of promise and opportunity, that Jared Potter Kirtland would eventually pursue his life as a prominent professor of medicine. It was in neighboring Rockport that he would make his home and pursue his studies of natural history.

Not long after joining the faculty at Drake's Medical College of Ohio in Cincinnati, Kirtland encountered Dr. Robert H. Collyer, a phrenologist. Seen from the perspective of today, Kirtland's relationship with Collyer is surprising. Kirtland's medical education was, for its time, outstanding. Not surprisingly, he set high standards for himself and his medical colleagues. Kirtland's private collection of books contained histories of Connecticut and Durham, where he had practiced for several years.[20] The former volume contains profiles of the region's physicians. Kirtland, as was his habit, added marginalia to the pages of this book. On page 192 the author wrote, "Dr. Moses Gaylord, who was a student in Durham with Dr. Cole, settled in Wallingford and became a distinguished surgeon." Kirtland commented, "For what? Quackery."

Despite skepticism and medical orthodoxy, Kirtland appears to have embraced phrenology—or at least allowed a practitioner of that pseudoscience that related personality to head shape to analyze his head. One must realize that phrenology may not have seemed so far from orthodox medical thinking at the time, however. Kirtland's personal library contained a text on this subject by Collyer, who described himself as "Professor of Phrenology (Pupil of the late Dr. Spurzheim)."[21] Johann Spurzheim was a German physician and one of the founders of phrenology. It is not clear that Collyer's credentials actually included an MD degree. Collyer was also a mesmerist who lectured and staged demonstrations of his alleged skills. Kirtland's copy of Collyer's book is inscribed, "To Dr. Kirkland [sic] with Dr. Collyer's Compliments. Nov. 24, 1838. Cincinnati Ohio." Folded and inserted into the back is a large certificate giving the results of Collyer's analysis of Kirtland's head. As was his frequent habit, Kirtland added penciled notes to many of the volume's pages; he had read the book with some attention to detail. These marginalia give insight into Kirtland's perception of his own personality. He was a gentle man, liberal, generally positive in outlook, but full of self-doubt.

In his notes, Kirtland portrayed himself as an optimist. "Misfortune soon forgotten," he commented. Collyer described him with the words, "Will give way to elevated and expansive ideas; will view nature through an immense magnifying power; ... will look down with pity and even contempt on all who take a more limited idea of things." "True to some extent," Kirtland commented. Collyer's text stated, "Values money merely as a means and not an end, only to carry on the affairs of life." "Fact," Kirtland noted, for he was, in his estimation, not materialistic. "Fond of seeing things in their place, but not observe order himself," Collyer indicated. "True," Kirtland wrote.

Kirtland felt he was a thoughtful person, but sometimes hesitant or timid. "True," he noted of Collyer's characterization as, "Very careful about his proceedings, seldom undertakes any thing without mature deliberation, and at times seems undecided and undetermined, lest he should do wrong, and when he has made up his mind, is afraid to carry out his project." In fact, Kirtland said of himself, "I have no confidence at all in myself.... [I] never very perfectly accomplish my purpose." He thought of himself as unable to "succeed when deep and original investigation is required" and often ineffective in expressing his ideas to others.

Kirtland was troubled by his poor memory for names, a common problem for the elderly, but not for those in their forties, as he would have been at the time. "I remember the person or object but soon forget the name," he wrote. And also, "I recollect events that occurred at 4 years of my age. Every battle that Bonaparte fought."

In one of Kirtland's most surprising comments he noted, "A distinguishing trait that has been the source of most of my troubles," in response to Collyer's phrenologically determined characterization: "Will be undecided, irresolute, and bend to the opinion of others; is so undecided in his manner as not to know his own mind.... Will conform to the ideas of others for the time being, and changes again when any new position is advanced by a second or third person—in fact he will lack energy or decision of character."

Kirtland thought of himself as kind and deferential to others. "True to the fullest extent," he noted of Collyer's description, "will not contend for his right; ... will be mild and amiable, and will surrender his rights sooner than contend for them, and will avoid quarrelling [sic]; he is tame and inoffensive; though, ... he may have shown himself off, and in the estimation of his friends appeared a brave man." Yet Kirtland considered true the statements, "Will express himself freely.... He will be frank, candid, and not much reserved.... He will not act with deception towards his friends," and also, "Always ready to oblige his friends.... Sympathizes with his friends in trouble and misfortune.... Kind and compassionate."

Not surprisingly, a love of animals emerged in those of Collyer's characterizations with which Kirtland agreed. "Hunt to obtain specimens in Nat. Science. Their suffering disturbs me," the increasingly eminent naturalist wrote. Collyer's words, with which he agreed, were, "will be extremely fond of hunting, and pride himself on his shooting; but ... will spare pain to the animals he may so destroy."

After his boyhood with his free-thinking grandfather, Kirtland was not sympathetic to organized charities and religious programs. Collyer wrote, "Will give to the support of missionaries and other religious purposes." "Never!" noted Kirtland.

Do Kirtland's self-deprecating reflections on Collyer's phrenology truly reflect his personality? Or are they the introspective thoughts of a man overwhelmed by his rapidly increasing responsibilities as a naturalist and about to embark on a professorial career for which he had little preparation? Or do they reflect some persistent depression after the deaths of his first wife and two children? Certainly Kirtland was highly respected in his community. His election to the state legislature for three terms of office attests to that. He could not have been withdrawn or reclusive. He must have been known, liked, and thought of highly by his neighbors.

The citizens of Trumbull County respected Kirtland for his medical skills. Moreover, his medical peers held him in esteem. He took a leading role in organizing the Ohio State Medical Society (now the Ohio State Medical Association), serving on a number of committees and as vice president in 1846. In 1848 he was elected to the presidency of the society. "Mild and amiable" in Collyer's assessment, perhaps, but a leader among his peers nonetheless.

Commenting on Kirtland's marginalia in Collyer's book, Patsy Gerstner, curator of the Dittrick Medical History Center, found the self-assessment revealed by these notes to be surprising for a man of Kirtland's stature.

> The most surprising elements to emerge from his statements concern a reticence, shyness, and self-consciousness not apparent in the force and direction evidenced by his achievements.[22]

Jared Potter Kirtland was a modest, unassuming man of easy temperament and liberal views. He did not assess himself as exceptional. Exceptional he was, however, in the eyes of his neighbors and colleagues. Exceptional he remains in the view of modern readers of the history of the Western Reserve.

6

Western Reserve University School of Medicine

Western medicine as a discipline, as a profession based upon a body of knowledge, had its origin with the Asclepiads, a guild of medical practitioners that originated on the Greek island of Cos. The greatest of these was Hippocrates, who brought his teachings to Greece during the fourth century BCE. Those who would practice this art studied with him and heeded his aphorisms, the first of which reads:

> Life is short; art is long; opportunity fugitive; experience delusive; judgment difficult. It is the duty of the physician not only to do that which immediately belongs to him, but likewise to secure the co-operation of the sick, of those who are in attendance, and of all the external agents.[1]

In this short and often-quoted statement, Hippocrates makes it clear that physicians are privileged in their practice and that they also bear responsibilities. They belong to a special guild. When assembled, Hippocrates's aphorisms constitute a remarkable text of medicine as he and his followers understood it. Throughout, he emphasizes the relief of suffering in the sick, a theme that also pervades Kirtland's teachings, as revealed in surviving letters and lecture notes.

Over the ensuing centuries, the education of would-be physicians was based on study with a preceptor. In this respect, medicine did not differ from other crafts. During the Renaissance, medicine flourished in universities. Distinguished medical scholars gave lectures attended by students who paid attendance fees to the speakers. Clinical knowledge and expertise were imparted during preceptorships with medical practitioners. This educational system continued well into the nineteenth century.

John Keats, one of the nineteenth century's outstanding romantic poets, was apprenticed to a local surgeon in 1811 at the age of fifteen. In 1815 he entered upon a one-year course of lectures and dissections at Guys Hospital in London. During that year he began writing poetry. His famous line, "A thing of beauty is a joy forever," first appeared on a page of notes from a lecture as, "A thing of beauty is a constant joy." Keats never practiced medicine. He chose to devote his short life to poetry.

This educational model—preceptorships combined with didactic lectures—became well-established in Europe and North America. Many skilled physicians emerged from this form of educational experience, including Jared Potter Kirtland. His clinical preceptorships in New Haven and didactic education at Yale and the University of Pennsylvania were exemplary for the time. Not all practitioners had this level of training. In fact, medicine prior to the mid-nineteenth century was largely unregulated, and many individuals with little or no education styled themselves as medical experts and advertised and practiced their trade without control or oversight.

Cult medicine and quackery flourished in nineteenth-century America. Hydrotherapy with cold-water showers was popular. Samuel Thomson of Vermont introduced a theory of herbal remedies based on the observation that the roots of plants reach into the earth and hence must bring sorrow and death, while leaves and shoots reach upward toward the heavens and so must relieve mankind's ills. He called his system of medicine Botanic Medicine; it soon became known as Thomsonianism. Thomson published a book describing his theories, and those who purchased the volume found it was accompanied by a certificate of membership in the Friendly Botanic Society and a diploma authorizing the purchaser to practice botanic medicine. A botanico-medical school opened near Columbus, Ohio, in 1839.[2] Kirtland denounced these aberrant forms of medical practice in his teaching.

The medical training of Daniel Drake, described previously, was typical of the time in Ohio. Qualified preceptors did not exist. Drake's mentor, William Goforth, was a self-appointed doctor without appropriate education. That he felt himself qualified to train Drake and to issue him a diploma was unremarkable at the time. Similarly, that Goforth's diploma was all the credentialing Drake sought or needed was within the norms of the day.

The opening of the Transylvania University School of Medicine in Kentucky in 1815 provided the first opportunity for Ohioans to undertake formal medical study. Easily accessible medical education came to Ohio in 1820 when, under Drake's leadership, the Medical College of Ohio in Cincinnati opened its doors to its first students. It was the second medical school founded west of the Appalachian Mountains, the thirteenth in North America. As noted previously, Drake's tenancy in Cincinnati was a stormy one, and the school there closed and then reopened.

Jared Potter Kirtland entered this changeable world of medical education in 1837. The course of instruction in Cincinnati was a series of lectures given by its six faculty members from November through February. The fees charged to the students included matriculation and hospital fees of ten dollars. Each of the professors received fifteen dollars, a total of ninety dollars, bringing the cost to each student to one hundred dollars.[3] Exact statistics are not available, but classes probably averaged about 100 students each year, which would have brought Kirtland an income of $1,500.[4] To the financially stricken Kirtland these funds would have been welcome.[5]

At this time Kirtland moved from Poland to Cleveland. Somewhat later he purchased a farm in Rockport. He spent the winters in Cincinnati but was free to return to northern Ohio each spring. As a result he could not have accepted apprentices from southern Ohio as other medical professors did.

Medical education in Ohio became more rigorous with ensuing decades. By 1875 some medical schools had instituted entrance examinations and preliminary education standards. By the end of the century, attendance at three medical sessions was the norm, and a few medical schools required four. For the most part, however, that meant simply repeating the course of lectures given each year. The number of schools operating in Ohio varied considerably, peaking in 1890 to 1891 at eighteen.[6] Currently there are eight medical schools in the state.

Willoughby, Ohio, is now an eastern suburb of Cleveland. Originally founded as Chagrin, it sits near the Chagrin River about fifteen miles from central Cleveland. The story of this community is intertwined with that of medical education in the Western Reserve and the life of Jared Potter Kirtland.

The early settlers of Chagrin came from central New York State in the vicinity of Fairfield. The first to settle in the area was David Abbott, who brought his family there in 1798 and recruited others to join him. Abbott was a Yale University graduate, and other early residents were also well-educated. Many of them traced their roots to the French Huguenots. They established a circulating library and organized a debating society. The first railroads in Northeast Ohio were built in the early 1830s, and one of them passed through the town. Hoping to establish their community as a center of education, the residents founded the Willoughby University of Lake Erie. They obtained a charter from the Ohio legislature on March 3, 1834.[7] The trustees voted to establish a medical department in October of that year.

From the start, the medical department was envisioned as having a central role at the new university. Initially, local physicians gave the medical lectures. Drs. George Card and George M. Henderson, leaders among the founders, recruited Dr. Westel Willoughby, then president of the Fairfield Medical College, to preside over the medical department. To spur Willoughby's interest in the position, they had renamed their town in his honor in 1835. Willoughby was wealthy and childless, and in changing the name of their community from Chagrin to Willoughby, the town fathers probably hoped that some of his estate would contribute to an endowment fund. He ultimately created a scholarship fund, but not a larger endowment.

Instruction began at the new medical school on November 3, 1834, and continued for a four month term. There were seven professors and three adjunct professors. Twenty-five students enrolled. The first few years of the new school were stormy, with faculty often absent and student enrollment low. A building for the school was completed in 1836 on two acres of land. A notice in the *Cleveland Herald* on July 29, 1837, reported:

> The college buildings will be in complete readiness to accommodate students. The dissecting rooms are ample and well equipped and a good Anatomical Museum will illustrate the course of the professor on that branch. Professor Cassels is

forming a General Museum. Sixteen hundred dollars worth of books is being added to the Library.[8]

The fortunes of the Willoughby Medical College changed in 1837. Not only were the buildings completed, but John Delamater came to the school as professor of surgery.[9] He was an effective leader of his professional colleagues, initially at Willoughby and later at the Medical Department in Cleveland of Western Reserve College in Hudson. Of French Huguenot stock, he was born in Chatham, New York, in 1787. He studied medicine with his uncle, Dr. Russell Dorr, for three years, obtained a medical license in 1807, and then joined his uncle in a practice in Chatham.

Somewhat peripatetic, Delamater practiced in several communities in eastern and central New York and western Massachusetts. Williams College, in Williamstown, Massachusetts, organized a medical department in nearby Pittsfield in 1823 that continued until 1867. Delamater joined its faculty in 1824, remaining for three years. He also served on the board of trustees of the school. Since he had no medical degree, Williams gave him an honorary MD in 1824. Leaving Massachusetts, he joined the faculty at the well-established and highly regarded Medical College of Fairfield, New York, as professor of surgery, where he served under Dr. Willoughby. His professorial appointments were in the theory and practice of physic, pathological anatomy, and obstetrics. While in Fairfield, he concurrently held professorships in several other medical schools, including Bowdoin in Maine and Dartmouth in New Hampshire.

Delamater recruited other physicians known to him to join the faculty at Willoughby. They comprised a cadre of distinguished physicians, and they soon vaulted the school into a position of academic strength. Delamater served as professor of materia medica, pathological anatomy, and obstetrics. Amasa Trowbridge was professor of surgery, Horace A. Ackley professor of general and special anatomy and of physiology, and John Lang Cassels professor of chemistry and pharmacology. The most distinguished of Delamater's newly recruited faculty was Jared Potter Kirtland, who served as professor of the theory and practice of physic and physical signs of diseases. In modern terminology, he would be called professor of internal medicine and physical diagnosis.[10]

Starting in 1837, Kirtland had been dividing his time between Cleveland and Cincinnati. The move to a professorship at Willoughby would have simplified his life, as he could have remained in his Cleveland home. The house he built at his Rockport farm was completed in March 1842, at which time he advertised his Cleveland house for rent. The winter term at the Willoughby medical school had ended by that time. However, when school resumed for the 1842-43 winter term at Willoughby, he must have faced a twenty-mile horseback commute to give his lectures. Perhaps he stayed with his daughter and son-in-law in Cleveland on many winter nights.

Two other Willoughby faculty members deserve note, as they joined Delamater and Kirtland in the later move to Cleveland. Horace A. Ackley was born in 1815 in the Finger Lakes region of New York. Little is known of his medical education. He began practicing medicine at the age of eighteen after attending lectures at the Medical College of Fairfield, New York. There he met Delamater, who would later recruit him to Willoughby. In Ohio he developed a reputation as a talented surgeon. In 1852 he was chosen to be the president of the Ohio Medical Society. His public persona was one of a brazen eccentric, with episodes surrounding his role in overseeing student anatomical dissections fueling this reputation. Plagued by alcoholism, he died of pneumonia in April 1859 at age forty-four.[11]

John Lang Cassels was born in 1802 in Scotland. He immigrated to western New York in 1827 and began studying medicine at the Medical College of Fairfield in 1830, receiving an MD degree two years later. Initially he practiced medicine in western New York, but in 1835 he joined the faculty at Willoughby as professor of chemistry. He had a major interest in geology, journeying not only in Ohio but also in Michigan's Upper Peninsula and Isle Royale seeking minerals. In 1861 he published a description and chemical analysis of a meteorite found in India.[12] He suffered a stroke in 1872 and died five years later.

Initial struggles at Willoughby gave way to success under the leadership of Delamater and Kirtland. The number of enrolled students increased; seventy students enrolled in 1842. Fiscally, the school struggled, however. On November 5, 1842, the *Cleveland Herald* editorialized:

> This School has been kept alive by individual exertion; and
> while the State has given many thousands of dollars to the
> Medical colleges in Cincinnati, not one dollar has it ever
> given to this Institution.... Justice demands of the Legislature,

that this School should receive aid at its hands. Let favors be equally distributed. We ask nothing more.[13]

In 1843 Kirtland, Delamater, Ackley, and Cassels resigned from Willoughby to take up professorships in the newly organized Medical Department in Cleveland of Western Reserve College in Hudson. Their departures followed the resignation and, shortly thereafter, death of college president Ralph Granger and the resignations of several trustees. Numerous dissensions are said to have arisen within the faculty, some of which may have been related to the use of cadavers for dissection that had been obtained by grave robbing.[14] Ackley was probably the leader of the four-man cabal that broke from Willoughby.

Willoughby's medical school struggled after the resignations of its most prominent faculty members and ultimately closed in 1847. An attempt to reorganize as a school of Ohio State University in Columbus failed. A seminary for women—the forerunner of Lake Erie College—occupied the former Willoughby building for nearly a decade before it was destroyed by fire in 1856.

The Western Reserve was settled by men and women from Connecticut who carried with them the Calvinist Puritan traditions that gave rise to Congregational churches. Sunday worship was important to them. After bringing his family to their new home, David Hudson erected a crude cabin as a church on the green in the new village that he and his party founded. It was the second church organized in the new territory of the Western Reserve. The first service was held on June 5, 1800.

There were no ordained clergy among the settlers, but from time to time visiting ministers from New England conducted services. Sunday worship could not be omitted when those men were not available, however. David Hudson, the leader of the community that would soon bear his name, assumed the role of deacon. He conducted worship services every Sunday.[15]

Few of the visiting New England clergy could be induced to settle in the Western Reserve. As early as 1801 a group organized as the Lake Erie Literary Society, with David Hudson as its president, petitioned the territorial legislature for a charter to establish a college at which young men could be trained as ministers. Their request was refused. In 1803 the legislature of the new State of Ohio reacted more favorably to the idea and granted a charter. An academy was organized and a building erected on land donated in Burton. In 1810 the Burton facility burned. It was rebuilt, but the program floundered and soon failed.

There was continued sentiment for the presence of an institution capable of training clergymen. In September 1821 the directors of the Portage County Missionary Society noted "the destitute situation of the churches in the bounds of the Society with regard to Ministers of the Gospel." The following spring the Presbytery of Grand River and Portage called for the "establishment in the Connecticut Western Reserve of a Literary and Theological Institution."[16]

With the Burton academy defunct, David Hudson led a successful campaign to raise $10,150 for the construction of a new college in Hudson. He himself contributed $2,142, the largest single donation and gave 160 acres for the school campus. After a political battle in the legislature—there were vociferous advocates for keeping the Burton location— a charter was granted in February 1826. On April 26 of that year the cornerstone of a three-story building was laid for what became known as Western Reserve College. In December 1826 the first three students enrolled.[17]

In September 1880, after two years of discussion, the trustees of Western Reserve College voted to move the institution to Cleveland, to a location adjacent to the newly founded Case School of Applied Technology. Amasa Stone pledged $350,000 to the effort, specifying that the name be changed to "Adelbert College of Western Reserve University." The following spring construction began on the forty-three-acre site of what had been the L. E. Holden homestead.[18]

As early as 1822, four years before Western Reserve College received its charter, those who advocated the founding of the college envisioned including a medical department. Seizing upon the opportunity presented by the defection of the four most prominent members of the faculty of the medical school in Willoughby, on August 4, 1843, the trustees of Western Reserve College authorized the professors from Willoughby to begin teaching medicine in Cleveland. They sought an amendment to their charter from the Ohio legislature, a move that was opposed by representatives from Willoughby. Kirtland traveled to Columbus and lobbied aggressively among the friends he'd made during his terms in the legislature in support of the new school in Cleveland. The legislature approved Western Reserve's request on February 23, 1844.

> Be it enacted by the General Assembly of the State of Ohio, that the Trustees of the Western Reserve College shall be and hereby are authorized to establish the medical department ... in the City of Cleveland, in the same manner and with like power to confer degrees and award diplomas as though the same department had been established ... at Hudson.[19]

On March 20, 1844, the trustees of Western Reserve College formally established the Medical Department in Cleveland.

Professorial appointments were made.[20] Jared Potter Kirtland stood at the head of the list as professor of the theory and practice of physic. His appointment was followed by John Delamater as professor of midwifery and diseases of women and children, Horace A. Ackley as professor of surgery, and John L. Cassels as professor of materia medica. There followed three additional appointments: Noah Worcester as professor of general pathology, Samuel St. John as professor of chemistry and medical jurisprudence, and Jacob J. Delamater (John Delamater's son) as lecturer on anatomy and physiology. An appointment as dean was given to John Delamater. Jacob J. Delamater and Ackley were appointed secretary and treasurer, respectively. Their terms of office were for one year, with faculty elections to be held annually to choose those who would continue in these offices. The minutes anticipated the early resignation of Worcester and subsequent reorganization into six departments. In fact, Worcester served only one year before resigning because of ill health. A board of censors was appointed, drawing its membership from local physicians. These men were charged with examining students at the end of the course of instruction to determine which ones would receive degrees.

In this and subsequent meetings, the trustees specified that the course of instruction was to begin on the first Wednesday of November and continue for sixteen weeks. Thirty lectures were to be offered each week, five by each of six professors. Diplomas were to be awarded in a ceremony on the Wednesday following the conclusion of the course of lectures. Students were to be charged a matriculation fee of three dollars and a graduation fee of twenty dollars. The fee for the course of lectures was set at seventy-two dollars, which was to be divided equally among the professors. Admission tickets to the lectures were issued to the students.

Sixty-five students entered the new medical school in November 1843. Most of them were Ohio residents, but the school also drew students from New York, Pennsylvania, and Michigan. Each was admitted to the course of lectures and assigned a clinical preceptor. These preceptors included not only faculty members, but also other physicians, presumably drawn from the community. Notably, Kirtland did not serve as one of these preceptors; all of the other faculty members did. His consulting practice in cardiology and pulmonary disease was centered in Rockport, where he also responded to requests from his neighbors for more general medical assistance. As in Cincinnati, geography made it impractical for him to take on trainees in his clinical practice. On July 23, 1844, after examinations, medical degrees and diplomas were awarded to twenty-five of the students at the end of the one-year curriculum. It is not clear whether the other forty did not complete the course or did not pass the examination. In the latter instance, they might have been reexamined and graduated later.

While these serious matters concerned the trustees, an entry into the minutes of November 5, 1844, contains a bit of levity for the modern reader.

> The subject of refunding promiscuously a medical student the amount of lecture fees, he having arranged for a course of lectures with Dr. Ackley by selling him as agent or Treasurer for the medical faculty, a horse—was introduced by Dr. Delamater, Sr. The subject was debated and it was considered improper to establish such a precedent but still the general expression was in the general favor of releasing him from his engagements until certain circumstances were communicated to the meeting, viz., that while he was applying to the faculty for a favor, he was representing to the medical students that the institution at Willoughby was much better qualified to

give instruction.... It was unanimously resolved that the faculty cannot interfere in the matter and that Mr. Blake has made a bargain and must abide by it. There was, however, a disposition to return the horse until Dr. Ackley informed the gentlemen that it had been disposed of.[21]

Aspiring students flocked to the new medical school. Cleveland, made prosperous by the opening of the Erie Canal and one year later the Ohio and Erie Canal, was growing in population and attracted young men who wished to become doctors. The medical school opened its first session with a lecture by Jared Potter Kirtland on Wednesday, November 1, 1843, at the Presbyterian Church located on Public Square on the site now occupied by its successor, the Old Stone Church. The general public was invited to attend.

Supporters of the Willoughby school challenged the new school. Local newspapers printed their assertions that degrees from it might not be legally valid. Detractors attempted to prevent the state legislature from amending the Western Reserve College charter to permit the school to be established and confer degrees. Kirtland's lobbying was instrumental in derailing these efforts. The Cleveland students joined the fray.

Students of the Cleveland Medical college assembled last night to answer those individuals "actively engaged in carrying out their designs to mislead uninformed persons," and adopted the following resolutions: That a majority of the physicians in the Western Reserve regard Cleveland as the only place in northern Ohio fit—because of size, situation, and commercial importance—for a medical school: that the present medical class, without an exception, are of the opinion that this institution is satisfactorily organized; that Professors Delamater, Kirtland, Ackley and Cassels did right in severing connections with the "Willoughby University of Lake Erie" which was in Notorious and intimate union with the "Ohio Rail Road Company;" that leading jurists have established the validity of M.D. degrees being conferred by Western Reserve college on students who have complied with the requirement of the Cleveland Medical College.[22]

The Medical Department of Western Reserve College, commonly known as the Cleveland Medical College, soon became firmly established and destined for rapid growth. The sixty-five students who entered the first class were followed in succeeding years by entering classes of 109, 160, 216, and 240. Following the demise of the school in Willoughby, matriculation increased further, peaking at 255 in 1849 and 260 in 1850.[23] This last number is substantially higher than the present enrollment at Case Western Reserve University School of Medicine.

Teaching facilities were needed. Initially, lectures were given in the upper stories of a commercial building in downtown Cleveland near Public Square at the intersection of Ontario and Prospect Streets. Drs. St. John, Cassels, and the younger Delamater were charged by the trustees with drawing up specifications for a building to house classrooms and lecture rooms, dissection rooms, and faculty offices. Faculty were assessed $300 each, to be paid in two annual installments. Funds from both the matriculation and graduation fees were designated for the building fund. Contributions were solicited and received from private donors. Attempts to obtain money from the state legislature proved unsuccessful.

The federal government had built a marine hospital on Lakeside Avenue east of present-day East Ninth Street to care for Great Lakes seamen. When a site near that facility became available at Erie and Federal Streets (now East Ninth Street and St. Clair Avenue) it was purchased for the medical school. Construction soon followed, and the building was ready for the third class of medical students to enter.

The new building was described in the *Cleveland Herald* in glowing terms.

> For its architectural beauty and commanding appearance it has perhaps not a superior in the state. It has three main stories besides a basement and attic, the whole surmounted by a spacious observatory.
>
> On the first floor are the general offices, and at the left, as you enter the building, is Professor Kirtland's study. The second main story is occupied by the library, the museum of the Academy of Science, and chemical apparatus.
>
> In the third main story the anatomical lecture room and anatomical museum can be found.

The lecture room is lighted from a dome in the roof.
Take the entire building from corner stone to dome, and
it is finished inside and outside with great skill and care.... No
College edifice in the Union equals this one.[24]

The Cleveland Medical College was not the only medical school in Ohio. During the mid-nineteenth century many medical schools arose in the state, varying in success and longevity. Some promoted medical cults. As noted earlier, a school in Worthington near Columbus promoted the vegetarian teachings of Thomson. It survived for only a few years. Homeopathic schools, including one in Cleveland, taught the principles of the oddly conceived idea that herbal remedies increase in potency with dilution. The Western College of Homeopathic Medicine opened in Cleveland in 1850 using the facilities at Ontario and Prospect occupied previously by the Medical Department of Western Reserve College. This building later burned. A homeopathic school for women existed for four years in Cleveland. Varying numbers of medical schools existed in Cincinnati.[25]

During the first two decades of its existence, there were changes in the faculty of the Cleveland Medical College due to resignations. But new professors joined the faculty, and the education of students continued without interruption. The 1851-52 catalog of Western Reserve College listed eighteen faculty members, of which six were medical faculty at the Cleveland Medical College. In an 1853 letter to W. H. Scoby, Kirtland reported, "Our school numbers about 170 students, a fine set of young men."[26] In 1852 the school awarded an MD degree to Nancy Clarke, probably the second medical degree given to a woman in the United States.[27]

In 1887 the original building was demolished and replaced with a larger facility. In 1924 the school moved to its present location in Cleveland's University Circle adjacent to the relocated campus of Western Reserve University (now Case Western Reserve University).

In April 1863, Jared Potter Kirtland offered his resignation to the trustees of the medical school. Because several other faculty changes were in process at the time, he was prevailed upon to stay. A year later, in June 1864, Kirtland, his health failing, asked to be relieved of his duties. His resignation was accepted.

In 1904 the American Medical Association and the Carnegie Foundation commissioned a survey of medical education by Abraham Flexner. Flexner, an educator, not a physician, visited all 155 medical schools then operating in the United States and Canada. In his 1910 report, Flexner ranked the schools. Sixteen earned places in his first division. It is clear from reading this report that Flexner considered the schools at Johns Hopkins University and Western Reserve University to be the two outstanding schools in America. Concerning Western Reserve he wrote:

> *Laboratory facilities:* Excellent laboratories, in which teaching and research are both vigorously prosecuted, are provided for all the fundamental scientific branches. A special endowment carries the department of experimental medicine. Books, museum, and other teaching accessories, all in abundance, are at hand. *Clinical facilities:* From the faculty of the school is appointed the staff of Lakeside Hospital, an endowed institution of 215 available beds, thoroughly modern in construction and equipment. The school has erected a clinical laboratory on the premises, so that close correlation of bedside and laboratory work is easily attainable. The relation of the two institutions has progressively become more intimate.[28]

Laudatory as it was, Flexner's report did not completely describe his impressions of Western Reserve University's School of Medicine. He wrote in a laudatory personal letter to Charles F. Thwing, then the university's president: "The Medical Department of Western Reserve University is next to Johns Hopkins University which, for various reasons, occupies an exceptional position, the best in the country."[29]

The medical school that Jared Potter Kirtland helped to found had become one of the leading medical schools in North America.

Jared Potter Kirtland at about the time he assumed his professorship at the Medical Department in Cleveland of Western Reserve College. Digital file in the archives of Case Western Reserve University. Reproduced with permission.

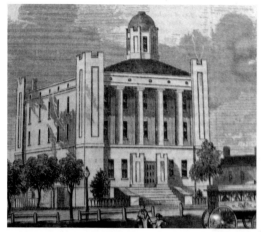

Original building of the Medical Department of Western Reserve College. Painting now hanging in Kirtland's restored house in Poland. Artist's signature is illegible. Photograph of the painting by the author. Used with permission.

Second building of the Medical Department of Western Reserve College. This contemporaneous photograph was used in newspaper advertisements and has been reproduced in many sources, including Frederick Clayton Waite, *Western Reserve University Centennial History of the School of Medicine* (Cleveland, OH: Western Reserve University Press, 1946).

Ticket of admission for a student to attend a lecture by Kirtland. Displayed at the Dittrick Medical History Center, Allen Medical Library, Case Western Reserve University. Photograph by the author. Used with permission.

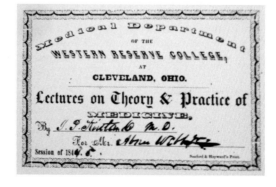

Portrait of Jared Potter Kirtland. *American Journal of Conchology*, 1867.

Kirtland's signature. From the flyleaf of a volume in Kirtland's personal library, now in the rare book collection of the Allen Medical Library. Photograph by the author. Used with permission.

Jared Potter Kirtland's Whippoorwill Farm house in Rockport. Archives of the Cleveland Museum of Natural History.

An elderly Jared Potter Kirtland in his garden. Archives of the Cleveland Museum of Natural History.

The Ark. Original building constructed by Leonard Case. Archives of the Cleveland Museum of Natural History.

David Hudson. Portrait by an unknown artist. This portrait dating from the early nineteenth century has been reproduced in many sources, including Wheeler, Robert A., ed., *Visions of the Western Reserve. Public and Private Documents of Northeastern Ohio, 1750-1860*. Columbus, OH: Ohio State University Press, 2000.

Western Reserve College in about 1890. The chapel seen at the left still stands and is used by Western Reserve Academy, which now occupies the campus. 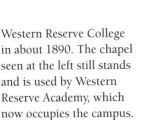 The original source of this early photograph is unknown. It has been reproduced in Clarence Henly Cramer, *Case Western Reserve: A History of the University: 1826-1976* (Boston, MA: Little, Brown and Company, 1976) and elsewhere.

Jared Potter Kirtland's house in Poland, currently restored and occupied. Photograph by the author. Used with permission of the current owner.

Becky Rogers manel et

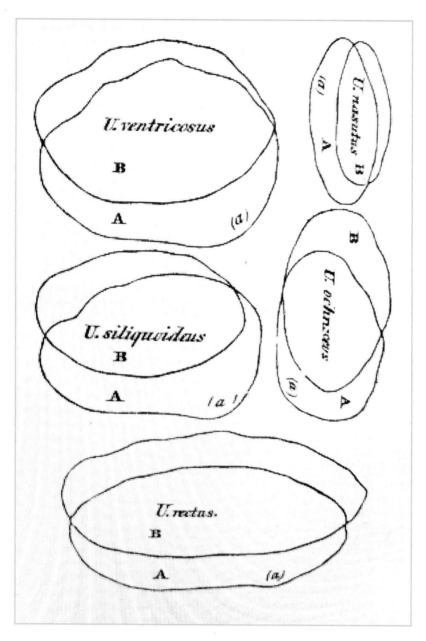

Jared Potter Kirtland's drawings of Ohio freshwater molluscs. *American Journal of Science and Arts*, 1834

Jared Potter Kirtland's drawings of four newly described Ohio freshwater fish species first recognized by him. *Boston Journal of Natural History*, 1840-1841.

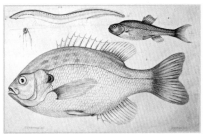

Kirtland's drawings of Ohio freshwater fish. *Boston Journal of Natural History*, 1840-1841.

Display case crafted by Jared Potter Kirtland containing bird specimens collected and mounted by Kirtland. Archives of the Cleveland Museum of Natural History. Photograph by Laura Dempsey, Cleveland Museum of Natural History.

Jared Potter Kirtland's specimen box and collecting scoop, now displayed at the museum of the Lakewood Historical Society. Photograph by the author. Used with permission.

7

Naturalist

During his lifetime, Jared Potter Kirtland became one of the most distinguished naturalists of the era. Well known locally, his reputation extended nationally. He was not, however, bred in one of the eastern universities that served as incubators for much of nineteenth-century American natural history. In his words, he belonged to:

> That class of self-made naturalists who attain to greater eminence than other[s] of equal talents and better advantages. Success in this branch of science requires not only a native genius but enthusiasm and never tiring perseverance; to the rich and educated these last qualifications are frequently wanting, or if not, instead of growing with the progress of life, they become more and more weak instead of more and more strong. Industry and ambition are more than a match for education in minds of the same order.[1]

In these words that date from late in his life, Kirtland enunciated the creed that had guided him through many years as he explored the world around him.

Jared Potter Kirtland's early talent as a naturalist became evident in the Connecticut orchards and gardens he tended for his grandfather. That part of the country had an important role in the silk production industry that had begun the previous century. Grandfather Jared Potter had an orchard of white mulberry trees, the leaves of which provide the principal food for silkworms. Young Jared Kirtland and his cousins were put in charge of this sericulture enterprise.[2]

Kirtland believed that female silkworms produced fertile eggs in the absence of male worms. He had observed this phenomenon—called parthenogenesis or asexual reproduction—in the course of caring for the silkworms. The young scientist followed up his ideas with experiments in which he isolated female worms from males. One of Kirtland's eulogizers described this accomplishment.

> With the co-operation of his cousins Jared managed this silk-worm culture, and there made the discovery that the female silk moth, without the male, could produce fertile eggs. This discovery preceded by nearly half a century the experiments and writings of Siebold on parthenogenesis in insects, and Steen's trap which demonstrated it.[3]

Kirtland's interests continued as he began his medical studies. In 1812, while a medical student, he marked items of special interest to him in an 1806 volume on gardening.[4] He drew small hands with pointing index fingers in the margins of this book. During the year when he studied at the University of Pennsylvania, he wrote a thesis on medicinal plants under the academic supervision of botanist Benjamin S. Barton. The thesis was titled "Our Indigenous Vegetable Materia Medica." While living and practicing medicine in Connecticut, he pursued his horticultural avocation.[5] He planted orchards and built a greenhouse.

Kirtland's years in Poland, Ohio, provided further immersion in botany and horticulture. In three years' time, Kirtland had developed an extensive inventory of fruit trees. The nursery he tended, however, appears never to have been a moneymaking venture. The 167 varieties of fruit trees and vines he offered to his local horticultural colleagues were given in the spirit of scientific discovery. As historian Rebecca Rogers notes:

> Kirtland seldom appears to have been in the nursery business. Rather, he shared his plants with "Amateurs of Horticulture" from whom he asked cuttings of choice plants not in his own garden collections. As Kirtland acquired more and rarer plants, often producing his own hybrids, he carefully wrapped cuttings with detailed instructions for cultivation

and declined monetary payment. From Ephraim Brown, in exchange for six varieties of grape, Kirtland requested "any variety of Flower or ornamental shrub, particularly fine varieties of Roses in Your Garden."[6]

Kirtland's interests were not confined to what he planted and cultivated on his land. He turned his inquisitive mind to the study of natural forms around him. Mussels from local streams caught his attention.

North America hosts the world's greatest number and diversity of freshwater mussels, with nearly 300 known species. Of these, eighty species have been known to occur in Ohio. They remain of interest to scientists today, primarily because of their sensitivity to pollution and, sadly, endangered status.[7]

Kirtland believed that previous descriptions of these invertebrates were inaccurate. In general, previous studies had concluded that these molluscs were asexual hermaphrodites. Kirtland found that separate male and female forms existed and that others had erroneously classified them as separate species. He carefully organized his observations and drafted a manuscript, illustrating it with meticulously executed drawings of five species. He submitted his work to the leading American scientific journal of the day, *The American Journal of Science and the Arts*, founded and edited by his former teacher, Benjamin Silliman of Yale University.

Kirtland began by noting inadequacies in the existing shell-based classification of mussels.

> In consequence of the characters, which are employed for scientific arrangement, in the systems of conchology, being derived, exclusively from the shells, the animals seem in a measure, to have been disregarded. Their general anatomical structure is not well understood: much less the intricate, and minute conformation of their sexual organs.[8]

He then reviewed previous descriptions of molluscs, citing specific published papers by well-known authors that he believed to have erred.

The leading authority on the classification of molluscs was Thomas Say. In the early nineteenth century, naturalists devoted much of their energy to the classification of the life forms they observed—taxonomy is the technical term. Say traveled widely in his studies of natural history. He was recognized as a leading taxonomist of invertebrates.

In 1830 Say published a work devoted to the shells of North America.[9] It included detailed illustrations drawn by his wife, who would become an eminent naturalist in her own right. Kirtland owned a copy of Say's book, and it is evident from the volume in his library that he studied it with care. Not originally paginated, it contains Kirtland's handwritten page numbers, as well as an index he added. Throughout Say's text Kirtland added marginal notes or marked items that must have been especially important to him. He had Say's work bound together with several other publications on mussels by Say and others—all indexed and annotated. Clearly, Kirtland carefully studied the existing work in the field of conchology before he expressed his own conclusions.

In his paper, Kirtland described his own studies and observations. He made specific comparisons of his observations with those that came before. He noted that in contrast to his predecessors, including Say, who had simply studied shells, he had studied the creatures' entire forms and their habitats.

> In the course of the three last years, I have dissected many hundreds of them, and carefully observed their habits, under a variety of circumstances, until I am persuaded, that the sexes are distinct, and that each sex, possesses a peculiar organization of body, associated with a corresponding form of shell, sufficiently well marked to distinguish it, from the other.
>
> The essential distinguishing mark of the female, discoverable in their internal structure, is the presence of ovaries, and oviducts.... To enable these viscera, to perform their natural functions without interruption, ... the shell is invariably somewhat produced, and varicose, more in some species than in others; and the posterior margin is generally truncated and inflated.[10]

Thus Kirtland concluded that the variations in shell configuration that had been used for species classification by Say and had been accepted by others were those variations necessary to accommodate sexual organs in the female and male forms of individual species.

Not surprisingly, Kirtland's report was not well-received by those whose work he had found to be erroneous. However, that it had been published in Benjamin Silliman's prestigious *American Journal of Science and Arts* gave it standing. Moreover, Louis Agassiz of Harvard University supported Kirtland's observations and conclusions. Few could challenge that endorsement, for Agassiz was the leading naturalist of the time. Kirtland demonstrated his collection of shells at the 1851 meeting of the American Association for the Advancement of Science in Cincinnati, Ohio. At this meeting he read a paper rebutting some of the criticisms that his published report had engendered. In the discussion that followed, Agassiz again came to his defense. In fact, over ensuing years Agassiz and Kirtland developed a close friendship and mutual respect. As for his critics and detractors, Kirtland later stated, "[they] had not waded our streams; collected and dissected the animals by thousands; nor watched their habits in their native waters and banks for years."[11]

Kirtland's interest in molluscs and their shells continued; his library contained a number of volumes by various authors on the subject. Some dated from the period when he was developing his thesis on the reproduction and classification of molluscs; others were acquired during later years. In 1858, more than twenty years after Say's death, his book was republished. Kirtland added it to his library. Following Say's death in 1834, Kirtland wrote of his continued respect for him in a letter to Samuel Hildreth.

> I participate with you, in most feelingly deploring the death of Mr. Say. The loss of no one, excepting of some near personal friend was ever laid so much to heart by me as that of this devoted amateur of science.[12]

Kirtland's meticulous, scholarly study earned him stature and recognition as a naturalist. Others soon came to heed his words, not solely for molluscs but for all aspects of natural history.

In the early nineteenth century, many of the country's adolescent states undertook surveys to better establish the natural resources of their territories. In 1836 the Ohio legislature laid the groundwork for such a survey when it appointed a committee to determine its particulars, including its cost. Ohio became the eleventh state to undertake such a project. Considering Kirtland's blossoming reputation as a naturalist and his past service in the Ohio legislature, it is not surprising that he was involved with this project from its inception. Not only molluscs, but all animal forms became Kirtland's responsibility during the Ohio Geological Survey of 1837. The year he spent on that project was singularly formative.

The state legislature authorized the survey on March 27, 1837. William W. Mather was appointed principal geologist; six assistants were named. Kirtland was put in charge of life forms as assistant zoologist. From the start, money was a problem. A national financial panic hit the country in May 1837, and this brought on a mood of financial conservatism that pervaded the legislature. Ultimately $16,700 was spent by the state, far less than was needed, and only one year of work was authorized. Kirtland responded to the financial constraints by forgoing his own salary and personally paying the salaries of his six assistants.

Kirtland was enthusiastic and ambitious as he approached his task. In the introduction to the report of his work, he described his plans.[13]

> The labor of collecting and arranging the productions of the recent animal and vegetable kingdoms of Ohio having been assigned to me, in the organization of the Geological Board, I proceeded to investigate the following classes of natural productions, viz: 1. Mammalia; 2. Birds; 3. Reptiles; 4. Fishes; 5. Testacea; 6. Crustacea; 7. Insects; 8. Plants.
>
> It was my first intention to make out a catalogue which might be considered perfect, embracing these several classes.

Kirtland further stated that he had intended to examine the specimens he collected against previous reports that might clarify their classification. This he found he could not do within the single year allotted by the legislature to the work. "Under existing circumstances, I hastened without delay to arrange my collections and make out catalogues." It is apparent that he did not sufficiently complete his work on insects and plants, for they are not mentioned further in his report. Following an introduction, Kirtland cataloged his specimens. He included fifty species of mammals, 223 birds, forty-eight reptiles, seventy-two fishes, 169 bivalve shellfish (testacea), and two crustaceans, a total of 564 species. At the end of the survey, Kirtland retained the specimens he had collected, ultimately adding them to a collection housed in the Cleveland Medical College.

During his fieldwork with the survey, Kirtland carried an 1820 book describing fish living in the Ohio River by Constantine S. Rafinesque, professor of botany and natural history at Transylvania University in Kentucky.[14] This work was evidently one of the prior studies with which he had hoped to compare his observations. Pasted into the back of this volume are Kirtland's handwritten notes on species that he found. Several of these inserted notes refer to discoveries made after the year in which the Ohio survey was conducted. Kirtland must have continued to use this book to record his field observations.

Kirtland's work on the 1837 geological survey of Ohio introduced him to two men who would be close friends and correspondents for the rest of his life. The first of these was Samuel Prescott Hildreth. He was born in 1783 on a farm near Lawrence, Massachusetts.[15] After attending Phillips' Academy in Andover and nearby Franklin Academy, he studied medicine with Dr. Thomas Kittredge of Andover and took a course of lectures in nearby Cambridge, Massachusetts. He received a diploma from the Massachusetts Medical Society in 1805. A year later he traveled west to Marietta, Ohio, where he began his practice of medicine and soon became the leading physician in the area.

Hildreth, like Kirtland, was interested in nature. Like Kirtland, he collected specimens of what he saw. Ultimately he donated several thousand of these to Marietta College. He had a major interest in the geology of the region in which he lived, and when the Ohio survey was organized he joined it as an assistant geologist. Hildreth lived until 1863, and throughout his life he and Kirtland kept up a lively correspondence.

The second of Kirtland's new friends was Charles Whittlesey. He was born in 1808 in Southington, Connecticut.[16] When he was seven years old his family moved to Tallmadge Center in Ohio's Western Reserve. After finishing his schooling there, he secured an appointment to the United States Military Academy at West Point in 1827. Graduating in 1831, he served in the Indian Wars as a brevet second lieutenant. He participated in the Black Hawk campaign of 1832. Soon thereafter he returned to civilian life. He too joined the Ohio survey as an assistant geologist. After the survey was completed, and while living in Cleveland, Whittlesey accepted commissions to survey several regions in the Lake Superior and upper Mississippi regions to assess their mineral ore potentials. His interests were broad, however, and he became an accomplished naturalist. He was appointed colonel of the Twentieth Regiment Ohio Volunteer Infantry and served with distinction during the Civil War. Thereafter he was commonly known by his military rank. He remained a close friend of Kirtland's, and served as a pallbearer at Kirtland's funeral.

Kirtland's national reputation as a naturalist grew with every scientific report he wrote—and there were many of them. Retired anatomy professor and medical historian Frederick Waite stated that more than 200 papers came from Kirtland's hand, although he could not locate many of them.[17]

Perhaps the most important of these, after his great work on molluscs, was his description of Ohio fishes, which derived from his work with the Ohio Geological Survey of 1837. Always eager to share his observations and discoveries with the wider community of naturalists, Kirtland prepared a description of four previously undescribed small fish and their habitats that he had found in the ponds and streams of the Western Reserve. It appeared in the *Boston Journal of Natural History*.[18] These fish ranged in size from one-half to three inches in length. Kirtland accompanied his descriptions of them with elegant, remarkably detailed drawings.

Kirtland followed his report of new species of fish in Ohio with an in-depth account of the fish he had observed during the Ohio Geological Survey of 1837. It was published by the *Boston Journal of Natural History* in a series of eight segments over a seven-year period.[19] Kirtland introduced his account by describing the origins of his study and its limitations.

During my connexion [sic] with the Geological Board of
Ohio, in the capacity of Zoologist, I directed my attention to

the fishes of the Western waters. The legislature of our state, changing its policy, discontinued our operations before any member of the Board had perfected his labors.

In this report I was unexpectedly called upon to make, I included a list of seventy-two species of Fishes, as inhabiting the waters of the Ohio River and Lake Erie and their tributaries, within the bounds of the State of Ohio.

Further investigations have enabled me to correct that list by expunging several that proved not to be true species, and adding others that had escaped previous observation.

The published account included descriptions of sixty-eight species of fish and detailed drawings of fifty-six species. Of them, eight represented species not previously described, including the four noted above.

Kirtland trod the meadows, woods, and streams of the Western Reserve as he collected an ever-growing number of specimens of the life forms he observed. He carried with him a metal collection scoop and specimen box that are now on exhibit at the Lakewood Historical Society Museum. He also received many specimens of interest from local friends and neighbors.

In late winter or early spring of 1850 Kirtland commented on the mild winters he usually experienced at his lakeshore farm in a letter to an unidentified eastern colleague. "A frost has destroyed all of the fruit at Cincinnati. Ours are safe and promise a great abundance."[20] In December 1851 Kirtland further commented on this phenomenon when he read a paper at a meeting of the Cleveland Academy of Natural Science entitled "Peculiarities of Climate, Flora and Fauna of the South Shore of Lake Erie in the Vicinity of Cleveland, Ohio." This paper was published the following March in the *American Journal of Science and the Arts* and also in the *Proceedings of the Cleveland Academy of Natural Science*.[21] In it he noted that his observations were made at a "locality ... situated five miles West of Cleveland," clearly referring to his Rockport home. Kirtland commented on the effect of the lake on temperature and seasonal changes. "During ... ten years the temperature has not often fallen below zero; while at Columbus, Marietta, and Cincinnati, situated from 120 to 150 miles South, it has frequently sunk to 5° [below zero]." While winter came late to Rockport, so did spring "as long as any considerable bodies of ice float upon the lake.... During winter," Kirtland noted, "comparatively little snow falls, and still less accumulates here, though it may be abundant on the higher grounds, thirty or forty miles in the interior." The lake-effect snow accumulation that Kirtland observed at higher elevations is well-known to today's inhabitants of Cleveland's eastern suburbs and Geauga, Lake, and Ashtabula Counties.

As one would expect, migrating birds caught Kirtland's attention. "Great numbers of [warblers] semi-annually congregate here, during their migrations, and seem to make it a resting place, both before and after passing the Lake."[22] Bird-watchers know this phenomenon today, and they journey to lakefront areas to observe these migratory species. Each year, International Migratory Bird Day is observed on the second Saturday of May at Magee Marsh and Crane Creek Beach on the lakeshore at the western edge of the Western Reserve.

Given the breadth of Kirtland's interest in natural history and that he collected specimens of all zoological life forms he observed, it is remarkable that no drawings of birds exist in his many publications and papers. In February 1837 he wrote to his friend and colleague, Samuel Hildreth.

> My studies during the past winter have been confined exclusively to natural sciences. I have reviewed and arranged what few subjects I have on hand, and also rearranged my shells— but any time when health & circumstances would permit has been principally devoted to Ornithology. I have attentively examined Audubon and Nuttal, particularly in regard to our winter birds and at the same time have been killing and stuffing specimens as rapidly as I could.[23]

Kirtland greatly admired Audubon's drawings. Writing of them to John Bachman, a naturalist who collected specimens for Audubon, he commented, "It is surprising that Audubon can give so much life and expression to [his subjects]. Perfect ... are the attitudes and contours of his birds."[24] Audubon used specimens mounted on wire frames as references for his work. However, Kirtland appears not to have employed this technique. In fact, there are no published drawings of birds that can be ascribed to him with certainty. Audubon did not preserve his mounted bird specimens but discarded them. Kirtland was an expert taxidermist and could easily have adopted Audubon's methods for drawing birds as well as preserving them.

Kirtland supplemented his preserved specimens with drawings, especially those of aquatic forms. His drawings of mollusc shells were key to his groundbreaking paper on their taxonomy. His drawings of fish were remarkably detailed. Kirtland's collecting is often associated with birds, perhaps because sophisticated birders know of the Kirtland's Warbler. His interests were eclectic, however. He shipped live snakes in cartons to several of his naturalist colleagues. He collected insects, preserving them in alcohol or sometimes in whiskey. He published detailed drawings of insects in the *Western Reserve Magazine of Agriculture and Horticulture*. *The Family Visitor* published his drawings of fish, and a few of insects. It also contains pictures of birds, but they lack the detail of his previous drawings, and some feature exotic species that Kirtland could not have actually seen.

In 1840 Kirtland became a member of the American Association of Geologists and Naturalists, an organization into which a number of societies devoted to natural science had coalesced. The group met irregularly, usually at yearly intervals, until it was formally organized as the American Association for the Advancement of Science in 1847. As the proceedings from the group's first session state:

> In conformity with a resolution of the "Association of American Geologists and Naturalists," adopted during its session at Boston, in September, 1847, that body agreed to resolve itself into the American Association for the Advancement of Science, and that the first meeting, under the new organization, should be held in the City of Philadelphia, on the third Wednesday (20th day) of September, 1848.[25]

To this day the AAAS is the global community of scientists' largest multidisciplinary society.

The proceedings of that first meeting in 1848 provide a list of members. Included is the entry "Kirtland, Dr. J. P., Cleveland, O." Kirtland kept a copy of these proceedings in his library. Ill at home, he did not attend the meeting. He remained active in the organization through 1857, after which he probably resigned. It was important in his life, providing a forum for interchange with other natural scientists. In his correspondence he referred to it as "the society." The 1852 meeting was scheduled for Cleveland, and it can be presumed that he would have chaired that session. However, a cholera epidemic raged in northern Ohio that year, and the meeting was canceled entirely. Instead, the 1853 meeting was held in Cleveland.

As further evidence of Kirtland's growing stature within scientific circles, in 1845 he was named to the original board of managers of the newly founded Smithsonian Institution. Arguably the greatest measure of Kirtland's national reputation, however, was provided by his membership in the National Academy of Sciences, which today is America's most esteemed multidisciplinary scientific society. Election to its membership is reserved for the most outstanding members of the country's scientific community. The academy is chartered by Congress but is an independent, nongovernmental organization that sets its own agenda. Today it functions largely by undertaking commissioned studies of scientific issues of major societal import. However, in its early years it was a forum in which its members presented and discussed their work.

The academy had its genesis at meetings of the American Association for the Advancement of Science, at which a group of academic scientists largely based at East Coast universities met informally to discuss their work and interests.[26] Dominating the group were Alexander Bache, a physicist from the University of Pennsylvania, and Harvard's eminent naturalist, Louis Agassiz. Originally coalescing in 1849, the group expanded and increased its prominence in the arena of American science. After a lobbying effort by some of the group's leaders, Senator Henry Wilson introduced in the Senate an act to charter the academy. It passed Congress on March 3, 1863, and was signed into law by President Lincoln.

As originally constituted, the academy consisted of a Class of Mathematics and Physics, chaired by Bache, and a Class on Natural History, chaired by Agassiz. Each class was divided into five sections. Membership totaled forty-four, all drawn from eastern university faculties. The first scientific meeting of the academy took place in January 1864 in rooms in the Capitol made available to it. This meeting was largely devoted to organizational matters. A second meeting followed in August. By the time of its third meeting in January 1865, several of the original members had died, and new members were elected for the first time. The first of these new members was Jared Potter Kirtland, who was elected on January 5, 1865, filling the seat made vacant by the death of his former professor Benjamin Silliman.

Kirtland's reputation as a naturalist led to many honors. Williams College in Massachusetts awarded him an honorary doctor of laws (LLD) in 1861. In 1875 he was elected to the prestigious American Philosophical Society, which had been founded in colonial times by Benjamin Franklin. Kirtland attended the March 7, 1867, meeting of the Conchological Section of the Academy of Natural Sciences of Philadelphia and was elected as a correspondent member of the academy at that meeting.

Some of the accolades Kirtland received might seem mundane or even silly. But honors they were. For example, his name was attached to a snake. It is a well-established convention among biologists that the one who first identifies and describes a new species has the privilege of assigning a Linnaean scientific name to it. First, one must identify the genus to which the new species belongs, or if the new species represents an entirely new genus, then that genus must be named. These names are Latinized, the possessive form used when appropriate to indicate relationship to an individual.

In 1856 American naturalist Robert Kennicott, who had studied medicine with Kirtland at the Cleveland Medical College, described a small water snake that he had found. This snake, limited to western Ohio, Indiana, Illinois, and neighboring regions of adjoining states, is today declining in number due to habitat destruction and is considered a threatened species in Ohio. Kennicott much admired Kirtland and named the snake in his honor. After some initial confusion, it is now recognized as a member of the genus *Clonophis*. Thus, *Clonophis kirtlandii* is its Linnaean name, and it is commonly called Kirtland's water snake. Kennicott died unexpectedly in Alaska in 1865 while on an Arctic expedition sponsored by the Smithsonian Institution. Kirtland's grandson, Charles Pease, was also a member of the expedition. He brought Kennicott's body back from Alaska.

In the nineteenth century many of those who could afford to do so turned to collecting, and among those items most treasured were specimens of natural history. Exotic life forms were the forerunners of today's "collectibles." Charles Darwin sailed from England on the *Beagle* two days after Christmas in 1831. The charge of the expedition he joined was to survey the coast of South America and Pacific Ocean islands offshore from that continent. He was the voyage's naturalist, and he collected specimens wherever he went—blue morpho butterflies in Brazil, birds in the Galapagos Islands, and many others from points in between. When he returned he had trouble finding resting places for his specimens. The storerooms at the London Zoological Society were full. A new museum on the grounds of the Royal College of Surgeons finally accepted his treasures.

American naturalist, ornithologist, and painter John James Audubon, best remembered for his monumental work, *The Birds of America*, was also a collector. He supported himself in large part by selling specimens. In England promoting his work, he urged his two sons in America to collect bird skins for him. Not skilled in taxidermy, he engaged an English taxidermist named Henry Ward in August 1831 to assist him by preparing the birds for sale or display. In the marshes near Charleston, South Carolina, Audubon and Ward shot, collected, skinned, and preserved 220 birds representing 60 species during one November week in 1831.

Collectors, including Darwin, went to great pains to preserve the specimens they collected. Taxidermy was a necessary skill. Kirtland honed his taxidermy abilities as he carefully preserved the skins of birds he shot for collection. He described the preservation of birds to a former medical student.

[The bird specimen] should be carefully skinned in the manner I showed the class. The flesh side should then be coated with Arsenical Soap or dry arsenic. The neck and head should be rubbed with the soap to make them turn back easy. The eyes and skull should be filled out just as full as natural with cotton.

The neck should have a little roll of cotton pressed into it on a small forked stick or probe but not as large as to distend it above its natural size. It had better be less.

Next fold the wings in place and put into the body a little ball of cotton about the size of the body. Smooth down all the feathers, tie the legs together and finally insert the skin, head foremost, into a paper cone like that formed by grocers to do up teas.

It will then dry and be ready to be softened down and mounted. Do not overfill the skin or stretch it in any way.[27]

Kirtland conducted a class in taxidermy. Many of the specimens that ultimately resided in his collections were prepared by the students in this class.

Starting in 1833, a group of Northeast Ohioans interested in collecting specimens from nature had coalesced around Kirtland. The group considered itself "a Lyceum ... which embraced the general discussion of popular subjects, in debates, lectures, and written essays."[28] Initially they met in a modest two-room frame structure built by Leonard Case, one of the group's leaders, adjacent to his house on the northeast corner of Cleveland's Public Square.[29] Later they met in Kirtland's medical school office. The building on Public Square became known as the Ark, because it housed so many animal specimens. The group called themselves the Arkites.

In 1858 or 1859 Julius Gollman painted a picture depicting the Arkites in their original building. The painting does not include Kirtland. Clearly visible in the upper right-hand corner is a display case containing specimens of birds. That case, measuring 18 by 24 inches and still containing its nine original bird specimens, is now archived at the Cleveland Museum of Natural History. While the museum's accession records do not indicate the case's original owner, accounts in the *Proceedings of the Cleveland Academy of Natural Science* provide substantial evidence that this case belonged to Kirtland. One can presume that he made it and that the birds it holds came from his collection.[30]

After an informal meeting of Arkites on November 19, 1845, which Kirtland attended with several of his friends and colleagues at the Western Reserve College Department of Medicine, a formal organizational meeting was held on November 24 to establish the Cleveland Academy of Natural Science. Kirtland was elected president of the new society. The academy occupied a room on the second floor of the Department of Medicine building in downtown Cleveland. More than half of the cost of refitting the room was raised by a "ladies fair."[31] The group's extensive collection of more than a thousand natural history specimens was exhibited there and open to public perusal. Many of the items in its collection were donated by Kirtland. The *Cleveland Herald* reported on this room.

> The center room is the museum, belonging to the Cleveland Academy of Natural Sciences. [It] is the most attractive room in the building to general visitors. The room is spacious and elegant, with four large pillars and lofty ceiling. Extending quite across on one side are five upright cases, containing at least one thousand specimens of foreign and domestic birds, and one case of animals.[32]

From 1845 through 1859 the academy published its proceedings. In addition to accounts of the society's meetings, the proceedings included letters to the academy from Kirtland, written during his travels and commenting on his observations. The proceedings also published letters written to Kirtland by Louis Agassiz and other eminent naturalists that Kirtland evidently felt would be of interest to the membership.

Not all of the natural history specimens to be found in the Cleveland Medical College were dead and stuffed. In a letter to Louis Agassiz, Kirtland wrote,

> My colleague, Prof. Ackley, has now in his possession a young wild-cat (Lynx rufus). It was captured on the Maumee River ... before its eyes were open. A house-cat adopted it with her brood. At length it was brought to our college and after a few days was set at liberty. It is now about four months old, is one third of its full size, apparently as tame and playful as a common domestic cat. At this time it is running at liberty about the Medical College and amuses itself playing with the students, disciplining the neighbors' dogs and capturing rats. When in a good-natured mood it manifests it by a loud purring - about as loud and musical as the sound of a spooling-wheel when in rapid motion.
>
> A few days since it became too familiar with a neighbor's hens. The owner shot it much to our regret.[33]

In subsequent years the academy withered, its members otherwise occupied, although its museum remained open. In April 1867 the society met again with renewed member interest. Once again, Kirtland was elected president. Two years later the members renamed it the Kirtland Society of Natural Science. Over the ensuing years the society again dwindled, and in 1926 the sole surviving member, Henry W. Elliott, gave the Ark's collections to the Cleveland Museum of Natural History, which had been founded in 1920.[34] In 1940 a Kirtland Society was organized at the museum, and under its auspices the Kirtland Bird Club, which remains active today. In 1976 the Kirtland Society was reorganized as the Kirtlandia Society. It continues as well, sponsoring monthly lectures on current topics in natural history.

Kirtland's interest in the world around him was not confined to Ohio and the Western Reserve. Not surprisingly, he traveled east to visit naturalist colleagues, sometimes tying these visits in with attendance at meetings of scientific societies. He made great efforts to attend the meetings of the American Association for the Advancement of Science. In August 1851 the association held two meetings, the second one convening in Albany, New York. Kirtland attended the meeting. In Albany he had hoped to meet Audubon, but failed to do so. From there he traveled to "Coney's Island" to collect specimens. He traveled to Washington, DC, in 1854, once again for a meeting of the AAAS. He extended this trip to Philadelphia. March 7, 1867, found him at a meeting of the Conchological Section of the Academy of Natural Sciences in Philadelphia. His expertise in this area was well-established by that time, and he was elected as a corresponding member of the academy at the meeting.

In 1853 Kirtland traveled west and north through Ohio, Michigan, Illinois, Wisconsin, and Ontario to explore the natural history of these regions and collect specimens. Joining him on these travels were Spencer Baird, a prominent ornithologist and ichthyologist and the first curator of the Smithsonian Institution in Washington, DC, and John Bachman, the South Carolina naturalist who had worked with Audubon. Bachman's major interest, however, was not in birds but in small mammals. In anticipation of the trip, he wrote to Kirtland, "If in Michigan we could get the small rodents, Meadow Mice and Shrews, I am sure we would get something new. I think we will add about fifty new species."[35]

In the spring of 1870 the then-seventy-seven-year-old Kirtland traveled to Florida accompanied by two members of his family: Charles Pease, his son-in-law; and Kelsey Cutter, his grandson-in-law, who was in poor health and hoped for improvement in a southern climate.[36] Kirtland was eager to visit this southern outpost of America and view its ecosystems so different from those he knew. The trip was originally planned to extend to Key West. He was to travel down the Ohio and Mississippi Rivers to New Orleans and thence to Florida. He expected to explore the St. Johns River from Jacksonville before continuing south. He considered this major expedition "a hazzardous [sic] undertaking for an imbecile of 77 years," but he did "not shrink from its dangers."[37]

His plans changed, however, and he traveled south by ship from New York. Encountering a major storm, he and his shipmates took refuge in Savannah, Georgia. Traveling on through the inland waterway by steamer he reached Jacksonville, where he chartered a "fine yacht." Exploring the St. Johns River, he enjoyed the tropical foliage and marveled at the midden mounds, which he surmised were evidence of prehistoric settlements. He drew drinking water from the river, disguising its brackish nature with juice from native oranges.

Becalmed in an inlet on Florida's St. Johns River, he wrote, "To the naturalist this is truly a wonderful country. At every landing new and beautiful wild flowers are discovered.... The Birds, Reptiles, Fishes, &c I am already familiar with by means of scientific works." Much of Kirtland's time on the St. Johns River was devoted to preparing and preserving the many specimens that other members of the party had collected

Kirtland's observations extended beyond Florida's natural history. At Mandarin he visited the "humble and beautiful" residence of Harriet Beecher Stowe, where his party was given a large supply of oranges. He found the post-Civil War Reconstruction period depressing. Educated and previously prosperous people suffered. A large number of "poor whites" he considered "ignorant, treacherous, and unreliable." He despaired of the future for Florida's African-Americans, whom he considered to be foolishly copying the lifestyles of uneducated whites. Kirtland was frequently a champion of those less fortunate than he. However, he was also a champion of individuals who were industrious, hardworking, and perseverant in the face of adversity.

8

Physician, Professor

When Jared Potter Kirtland took up his responsibilities at the newly founded Medical Department of the Western Reserve College at Cleveland in 1843, he assumed the position and title of Professor of Theory and Practice of Medicine and Physical Diagnosis. In fact, in this role he then functioned as the entire department of medicine.

Not surprisingly, it fell to him to give the opening lecture at each annual session. In 1848, Kirtland's fifth year in Cleveland, a student committee requested his permission to publish his introductory lecture.[1] This lecture was not devoted to platitudes about the responsibilities of physicians, the subject of many of today's medical school opening sessions and also of many medical school commencement addresses. Rather, it leapt directly into the treatment of disease, focusing on the unexpected, often harmful effects of many remedies then current. It also denounced practitioners outside of the orthodox medical establishment. But not before a grandiose opening.

> From that momentous period, when man's first disobedience,
> "Brought death into the world, And all our woe," down to the
> present, pain and disease have afflicted the human family. The
> profession of medicine must have originated, as a conse-
> quence, coeval, perhaps, with that great event; the practice
> has called forth the efforts of the learned, and ignorant, wise,
> and unwise, regular, and irregular, of every age, in the pursuit
> of one common object, the discovery and application of
> means for the relief of suffering humanity.

"Remedies," Kirtland noted, "under certain circumstances, will counteract disease." Sometimes, however, remedies may "coincide, ... to augment or modify it ... into a more malignant form." He cited the harmful effects of alcohol, capsicum, and quinine given to patients with "sthenic" (abnormally and morbidly hyperactive) illness. He similarly faulted neutral salts, antimony, and "the lancet." That he included the lancet—i.e. bloodletting—bespoke his moderation with this practice commonly employed by most doctors at the time. "Remedies will coincide if not adapted to the grade of disease."

Departing from remarks on specific therapies, Kirtland commented on various theories and systems of medical treatment. He castigated quacks, who "never grow wiser or better, except in their own estimation." Hydrotherapy, which called for patients to be subjected to cold-water showers, was "attended with danger." Homeopathy's remedies he called, "mere nullities ... [that relieve] symptoms by the operations of the imagination—the only medium through which it ever acts." Furthermore, "it is unsafe, under any circumstances, to employ secret nostrums," and "quacks, empirics, and irregulars of all denominations, are not qualified to practice medicine with safety."

Kirtland's lecture read in toto is a plea for orthodoxy and moderation. He embraced most of the current therapies in medical practice but cautioned against their inappropriate or excessive use. And he denounced practitioners who operated outside of the arena of conventional medicine and the teachings of medical school professors.

Initially Kirtland wrote out his lectures in full and read them. As he became more experienced, he simply kept an abstract or outline of his subject before him and spoke extemporaneously. Thus he established contact with his students in the classroom. While his office was always open to students, he kept a sign posted on the wall beneath the clock reading, "Time is money. I have neither to spend except for useful purposes."

As one would expect of the leading practitioner of medicine in the Western Reserve, a professor of medicine, and a man who had a classical education and enjoyed reading, Kirtland had an extensive library. Contrary to expectation, however, this library did not contain a substantial collection of medical works. Kirtland inherited his grandfather's medical books. During the course of his education at Yale's and the University of Pennsylvania's medical schools, he certainly would have studied the leading medical texts of the time. Yet his personal library contained a remarkable paucity of medical books. Most of the volumes in his collection dealt with natural history.

In 1900, twenty-three years after Kirtland's death, his granddaughter, Caroline Pease Cutter, donated his papers and books to Western Reserve University. A catalogue of this collection compiled in 1966 includes 298 items. Only three are medical works: two devoted to physiology and one to herbal remedies. The large remainder is divided roughly equally among books and papers devoted to natural history, accounts of travel and exploration, and works devoted to horticulture. It appears that Kirtland was more interested in his avocations as a naturalist and agronomist than his profession as a physician and professor, at least in his later years.

A handful of works bearing Kirtland's distinctive bookplate but not included in the catalogue of those donated by Caroline Cutter reside in the historical collections of the Allen Medical Library of Case Western Reserve University. Dealing with various aspects of medicine and medical therapy, they number no more than a dozen. Early publication dates suggest that some of them came from the collection of Grandfather Dr. Potter Kirtland. If these medical publications were not erroneously omitted from the catalogue of those donated by Cutter, it is likely that they were given to the Cleveland College of Medicine library by Kirtland himself, perhaps at the time of his retirement from the faculty in 1864. This was certainly true for *The New Edinburgh Dispensary* by William Lewis and for *The Surgeon's Practical Guide in Dressing* by Thomas Cutter, for these two volumes contain bookplates noting that they were donated to the medical library of the medical college. Two volumes on venereal diseases with publication dates of 1767 and 1797 were probably among the books Kirtland inherited from his grandfather. A text entitled *Elements of Therapeutics and Materia Medica* by Nathaniel Chapman contains bookplates for both Kirtland and John Delamater. Delamater retired before Kirtland, perhaps passing this book to him at that time.

The sparseness of Kirtland's medical library should not imply that his practice of medicine was lacking. Medicine at the time was largely empiric and experienced-based. Beyond attending lectures at Yale and the University of Pennsylvania, Kirtland learned clinical medicine from those clinicians with whom he served clinical preceptorships. Additionally, Kirtland's extensive personal experience in treating the diseases common in his practice added to his medical knowledge.

On January 3, 1843, the *Cleveland Herald* carried a notice that read:

> Dr. J. P. Kirtland has opened an office ... where he will investigate important cases of chronic diseases and make prescriptions. Particular attention will be paid to consumption, affections of the heart, and other diseases of the chest, the character of which he examines by the stethescope [sic] and the aid of physical signs.
>
> He will also visit patients, but only in the capacity of counsellor [sic] and in company with their attending physician, to this rule there will be no exception.[2]

At this time Kirtland was a professor at the Willoughby Medical College. As the newspaper notice indicates, Kirtland considered himself a consultant, an expert with standing above that of most medical practitioners of the day. This self-assessment was not inconsistent with his professorial status at Willoughby and subsequently at the Cleveland College of Medicine. He believed his professorial role marked him as more highly qualified than other doctors.

The announcement of the opening of Kirtland's medical office provides several insights into the man's character and professional status. First, he sought to augment the income he garnered from teaching medical students. Kirtland was not a wealthy man, yet he lived comfortably on his Rockport farm. His father, Turhand Kirtland, had given him land and a house in Poland as well as bank stock. Turhand died in August 1844, a year following this newspaper notice. Kirtland's mother died six years later. He might have shared in their estates, but not by the time of this announcement. He spent money on his naturalist activities, which were of great importance to him. Indeed, one cannot help but suspect that he might have preferred to devote all of his energies and resources to natural history, had he not needed the income from his medical profession.

A modest man, we are told, yet here he presented himself not only as willing to see patients in his office but also to serve as a consultant to other physicians and a specialist in heart and lung diseases. Thus, he must have believed that his clinical skills and his status as a professor would lead other practitioners to seek his advice and assistance with particularly challenging clinical problems in their patients. When he advertised his willingness to serve as a consultant, he stated that he would accept consultation requests only from another doctor—not directly from patients—which accorded with medical ethics and practices of specialists of that era. That he advertised—the announcement in the *Herald* was probably a paid notice—was also acceptable and common practice in his day, though later it was frowned upon by the stalwarts of organized medicine. More recently, paid advertising by physicians has come back into practice.

Despite Kirtland's obvious wish to position himself apart from the general practice of medicine, he continued to provide general medical care for his friends and neighbors in Rockport. His letters repeatedly offered medical advice to relatives with whom he corresponded. He was at heart a man who was generous with his knowledge and in no way autocratic.

Remarkable in the *Herald's* notice is that Kirtland offered to examine patients with a stethoscope. At the time that Kirtland opened his office, diagnosis with a stethoscope was a recent advance and at the cutting edge of medical technology. It was equivalent to diagnosis with an MRI or PET scanner today. Kirtland was not a simple country doc; he was a specialist. And he was a specialist at the leading edge of medical technology. The stethoscope was invented by René Théophile Hyacinthe Laennec in 1816. It bore faint resemblance to today's instruments. It was a simple wooden tube, flared at one end into a bell that could be placed against the patient's chest and shaped at the other end to fit an examiner's ear. Simple, perhaps, yet effective. Laennec installed a lathe in his Paris apartment to produce his instruments. He first described his stethoscope publicly in 1818 and published a text in which he laid out its capabilities for examination of the lungs the next year. A careful drawing of the instrument was included in the book. Laennec's French text was revised, edited, and translated into English by John Forbes, a London

physician with special interest in respiratory diseases, in 1821.[3] Thereafter, stethoscopes rapidly came into use in Europe, and many leading
practitioners traveled to Paris to be instructed in its use by Laennec.
When and how did Kirtland learn to use a stethoscope? Did he
make his own instrument? We cannot know the answers to these ques-
tions, but we can make some reasonable assumptions. Kirtland's library
contained an 1839 volume by Charles J. B. Williams entitled *Lectures on
the Physiology and Diseases of the Chest Including the Principles of Physical and General Diagnosis*.[4] In his work Williams describes Laennec's
stethoscope and discusses its fabrication and the best woods for it. He
does not include an illustration, but refers to another of his works,
which Kirtland did not own. Williams recommends a turner in Philadelphia skilled in the manufacture of stethoscopes. Perhaps Kirtland obtained his instrument from this source, or perhaps a local woodworker
was able to fabricate an instrument from Williams's description. We
must assume that Kirtland learned much about the use of his stethoscope empirically, although Williams's book discusses the signs of lung
disease that can be elucidated with it in some detail. Williams reviews
the relevant observations of Laennec and credits his work.

Consumption (tuberculosis) headed the list of diseases to which Kirtland directed his attention. It was a common affliction in North America and Europe at the time and one with ominous consequences. Specific
data for the Western Reserve are lacking, but in a scholarly analysis
E. R. N. Grigg states that the death rate in Ohio in the mid-nineteenth
century was approximately 200/100,000/year (current American death
rates for tuberculosis approximate 0.2/100,000/year).[5]
  Kirtland's views on tuberculosis are expressed in his surviving handwritten lecture notes. When considering them, however, it is important
to understand the state of knowledge of this major source of illness at
the time. Three words were used to describe the disease. *Phthisis*, derived from a Greek word meaning "to wane," denoted pulmonary disease. *Consumption* referred to disseminated disease characterized by
wasting and an invariably fatal outcome. (Some people characterized as
consumptive probably had some other fatal, malignant disease, but tuberculosis certainly predominated for those persons not yet in their

elder years.) Finally, *scrofula* referred to tuberculosis of the lymph nodes. Laennec had established that these three illnesses were, in fact, all manifestations of tuberculosis. His monumental, classic work not only elucidated the pathology of pulmonary tuberculosis but, as previously noted, also described his newly invented stethoscope.[6]

The treatment of tuberculosis in Kirtland's time was symptomatic. Sanatoria offering rest treatment specifically directed at the disease would not appear for another half century. To establish the context of Kirtland's approach to tuberculosis, it is useful to compare his statements with contemporaneous texts on the subject. The work of Charles J. B. Williams provides an apt representation of medical knowledge and thinking about the disease at that time. Williams was an English physician of considerable note who specialized in treatment of lung diseases and was considered an expert on tuberculosis. His lectures were published in 1839, and as noted previously, Kirtland owned a copy of this text. Williams was moderate in the therapy he advocated, focusing on measures to "diminish those local irritations ... that lead to the formation of tubercles."

Kirtland's library included a 1796 book written by Thomas Hayes, a London physician and surgeon, published in Boston.[7] When Kirtland acquired it is not evident, but the publication date suggests it may have come to him from his grandfather's library. It is inscribed by Kirtland, suggesting that he did more than simply put it on a bookshelf. As it is the only work surviving in his library that is specifically directed at tuberculosis, it may be particularly relevant to Kirtland's teachings.

Hayes wrote that in agreement with the "late Sir John Pringle, a distinguished ornament of his profession, consumptions ... are almost always owing to neglected colds." He clearly embraced heredity and physique as disposing to tuberculosis. Those "such as are tall and thin, with long necks, flat chests, and with shoulders sticking out like wings, and otherwise of a delicate texture, are the most common victims to consumptions." For the treatment of tuberculosis Hayes recommended inhalation of vapor from salt water, a long litany of herbal decoctions, and blistering—"small ones to be applied from time to time to different parts of the chest." He prescribed a restricted diet. "Flesh meats ... must be forbidden.... Fruits, vegetables, milk and farinaceous substances" were recommended. He advocated walking and riding early in the morning. In company with most authorities of his time, he also recommended blood-letting. "Nothing stops the progress of inflammation so much as bleeding, from six to ten ounces of blood may be taken away immediately."

Kirtland's surviving lecture notes on tuberculosis lack their initial paragraphs, perhaps one or two pages.[8] The bulk of the notes remains intact, however. Kirtland classified tuberculosis into three stages, evidently beginning his discourse with consideration of the late and severe third stage, which was noted as "tubercular consumption." He viewed this stage as ominous, and, it is worth noting, he distinguished the wasting and disseminated disease of tuberculosis from other conditions such as cancer. The second stage Kirtland defined as that "after it has involved the lungs."

> The prognosis is ... unfavorable, yet we should not still despair of success. I have known the ulcerations of the lungs in such cases to heal rapidly under the influence of a slight course of mercurials, expectorants & opiates, together with change of climate or suitable exercise.

The first stage, in Kirtland's classification, was that of "predisposition." It is clear from his notes that Kirtland shared the prevailing opinion of his medical contemporaries that this predisposition was hereditary.

> Persons thus predisposed should conscientiously abstain from matrimonial connections but as they will not it will be your duty to endeavor to counteract the evil as much as possible. Their children may by suitable case be rendered strong and healthy. This must be done by attention to diet, sleep, exercise, amusements & mode of education.
>
> Instead of nursing them as sickly and weakly beings ..., it should be our endeavor to draw out to maturity the physical powers & the mind should be left to expand as a consequence of discipline....
>
> They must have a sufficiency of nutritious matter but it should be of the simplest character.... Such children should if possible be placed in the country on a farm & be allowed to exercise without restraint & if possible be made to work occasionally though not beyond their strength.

Clothing for those in this stage of predisposition, Kirtland noted, "should be regulated by the weather." He recommended frequent but moderate exercise and saltwater baths. He emphasized comfort for his consumptive patients. Masturbation, he commented, was a cause of tuberculosis among young people.

It was common to classify tuberculosis, and that practice continues today in relation to its infectiousness. Williams did so in a logical order of ascending severity, but he restricted his classification to manifest disease. He did not including Kirtland's "predisposition" stage.

Kirtland discussed some of the commonly employed contemporary therapies for tuberculosis. Vesicants and other irritants were applied to the chest by many practitioners. Williams and Hayes both recommended that cream of tartar be applied to the chest. Williams also recommended a lotion containing vinegar, salt, and turpentine with specific instructions that it be "rubbed in below the clavicles twice a day." Kirtland believed counterirritation to be "one of the most successful modes of countering the approach of this disease." He further stated:

> It should be recollected that it is often more advantageous to stimulate and act upon the base of the nerves that supply the organ than endeavor to make the toxic impression in the contiguity of the organ itself. In this case counterirritants will often do more applied to back of the neck and spine than to the thorax anteriorly.

The mainstays of nineteenth-century tuberculosis treatment were blood-letting and sea voyages. When John Keats developed tuberculosis in 1820 the physician who first saw him immediately withdrew blood from his arm. A decade and a half later Chopin's physicians bled him. As a young man, George Washington accompanied his half-brother Lawrence on a voyage to Barbados when the latter was afflicted. Kirtland stated that both blood-letting and sea voyages could be helpful, but he devoted little attention to these therapies. "In certain cases particular[ly] those of a hemorrhagic disposition it is often advisable to take small quantities of blood from the arms to prevent the attack on the lungs." It appears that Kirtland envisioned the disease as a blood-borne, evil humor-mediated inflammation, a concept with origins in earlier medical times. It is notable that he speaks of "small quantities of blood" in "certain cases." Other practitioners used blood-letting aggressively at that time.

Pharmacologic agents for treating tuberculosis in Kirtland's time emphasized cough suppression, sedation, and pain relief. They commonly included opiates, which are effective in this regard; their derivatives are used for cough suppression today. In his text, Hayes endorsed a number of herbal medicaments. "I recommend decoctions or infusions of liquorice root, figs, and raisins, marsh mellows, dandelion, colts foot, comfrey, eryngo and mullen [sic] roots." Although Kirtland was an expert horticulturist and herbalist, his lecture notes make no reference to plant-based pharmacologic agents.

Recalling that Kirtland denounced stimulating medicines as "coinciding" for sthenic illnesses (illnesses characterized by hyperactive responses—rapid pulse rate, for example), his recommendations for the use of counterirritants and vesicants seem questionable. However, tuberculosis rarely presents as a sthenic condition until the patient is near death. Rather it is an asthenic one, for which Kirtland would have considered these measures appropriate.

Kirtland owned a publication espousing the inhalation of various substances, some of which seem bizarre to the modern reader.[9] This text described the benefits of inhaling air enriched with oxygen. A detailed description of equipment for generating oxygen was included. The book has a publication date of 1795, suggesting that it too might have been inherited from his grandfather. For his part, Kirtland endorsed the inhalation of "the vapors of tar" for the treatment of tuberculosis.

Knowing the views on tuberculosis that Kirtland presented in his lecture notes, it is interesting to consider a letter he wrote on October 10, 1851, to Sarah Boardman, whom he addressed as "Dear Friend."[10] Her communication that prompted this letter in reply has not survived. It almost certainly asked for advice about an individual recently given a diagnosis of tuberculosis following an episode of hemoptysis (coughing or spitting of blood). After explaining his inability to travel to see the patient, Kirtland wrote:

One of the great advancements in modern practise [*sic*] is the discovery that in consumption, hemorrhage and tubercles of the lungs and in all varieties of scrofulous disorders, the action of the system is of an <u>atonic</u> or weakened condition of the system. Even if in the progress of disease, disorganization of any structure should ensue, the lungs, for instance, as in consumption, the inflammation attendant upon it, is also of <u>atonic</u> <u>character</u> and not <u>phlogistic</u> or in common parlance <u>inflammatory</u>.

With this view before us - i.e., that <u>hemorrhage</u> <u>of</u> <u>the</u> <u>lungs</u> <u>and</u> <u>a</u> <u>tendency</u> <u>to</u> <u>the</u> <u>formation</u> <u>of</u> <u>tubercles</u>, the indication of cure to be pursued is - <u>to</u> <u>raise</u> <u>the</u> <u>standard</u> <u>of</u> <u>the</u> <u>system</u> <u>above</u> <u>that</u> <u>atonic</u> <u>condition</u>.

With this indication we, of course, should avoid everything that will in any way reduce the system - bleeding, antimony, cathartics, emetics, depression of spirits, etc. On the other hand, we should employ means calculated to raise and invigorate the system, done to the individual case. This, I am aware is directly in opposition to the views entertained in former times, when a hemorrhage of the lungs was supposed to be connected with an active inflammatory state of the system and the danger apprehended was that inflammation would follow in the lungs and ultimately result in the formation of ulcers in the lungs.

This old view is entirely exploded by the discoveries as to the formation and nature of tubercles and the progress of consumption made in recent years by pathologists.

What should then be done with a case of hemorrhage of the lungs and a tendency to the formation of tubercles is a question that will probably be asked. I will answer it.

1st. Avoid all violent means, all agitations, loud speaking, severe fatigue, all reducing medication, such as foxglove, antimony and blood letting—also blistering. Keep the patient, when indoors, in a large well-ventilated room. Let him be out in open air as much as possible, guided by his strength, but by no means shut him up in a sickroom.

Let him use daily as much Old French Brandy, Jamaica Spirit, Porter, Ale, or perhaps Madeira Wine as the system will tolerate, without disturbing the head and raising an uncomfortable state of fever.

Wash the whole surface of the body morning and evening with alcohol in some form and either cold or tepid as best suits the feelings of the patient.

The diet should be generous and full, the quantity to be regulated by the powers of digestion. A full moiety should be animal food, either fresh or salt to suit the appetite. Avoiding pastry, pickles, vinegar and indigestible vegetables such as beans, cabbage, etc. Farinaceous vegetables, potatoes, rice and ripe fruit may be used.

In addition to the above <u>Rectified</u> Cod Liver Oil should be employed twice or thrice daily in doses as the stomach and bowels will bear, say 1 teaspoonful at first. Keep the body and mind active and vigorous as possible.

This course is directly in opposition to all old-fashion views but I must assure you it is not merely theoretical. I can point to very many living individuals who have recovered under the above plan of treatment. I have been testing it for the last 10 years with great success.

Still in the hands of those who may retain a predilection for the old and fatal modes of treatment I fear it would not be faithfully carried out. I however deem it to be a matter of duty as well as an act of friendship to give you my views.

In a postscript Kirtland added:

Permit me to add that the above mode of treatment is like a chain—the omission of one single link will break it. Also the attempt to modify it by a mixture of some of the old reducing plan will be equally objectionable. Oil and water will not mix.

Except that Kirtland had replaced terms such as "asthenic" with "atonic," the recommendations included in this letter are consonant with those of his introductory lecture to medical students. Since Kirtland's tuberculosis lecture notes are undated, it is not possible to know how much time elapsed between their origin and the letter to Sarah Boardman. It might have been ten years. The lecture notes show evidence of some revisions, but they were not major. During whatever time ensued, Kirtland's approach to tuberculosis moved from one that was customary for the era, albeit somewhat liberalized, to one that espoused minimal therapeutic manipulation. Notably, the Boardman letter did not recommend bloodletting. His ideas anticipated by many decades the outdoor life regimens that came with the sanatorium movement at the end of the nineteenth century. At the same time, he continued to believe that his recommendations must be followed explicitly without modification—just as did sanatorium doctors during their therapeutic reign.

The views Kirtland expressed on the pathology of tuberculosis at the start of this excerpt of the Boardman letter are in agreement with the findings of autopsies presented by Laennec and probably espoused by later pathologists with whom Kirtland may have had contact. They reject the acute inflammatory concept of this disease and recognize the central role of granuloma formation, a more chronic tissue reaction.

Kirtland's thoughts on the infectiousness of tuberculosis were foresighted and at variance with what was generally held by the medical profession at this time. In 1890 the *Cleveland Medical Gazette* editorialized in a tribute to him, "In the note-book of a student who attended lectures in the winter of 1856-57, we find that Professor Kirtland thought and taught that *phthisis is contagious.*"[11]

Kirtland's moderate views on the treatment of tuberculosis were held by many leading medical experts of the time. Williams's 1844 text emphasized measures to overcome "constitutional weaknesses." "Pure country air," he wrote, "is almost indispensable to give any chance to the consumptive." Williams seemed more ready to employ blood-letting than Kirtland, although he cautioned against its excess use. Williams referred to Sir James Clark, Britain's leading lung specialist and physician to Queen Victoria. Clark, who treated John Keats, held moderate views on the treatment of tuberculosis and on blood-letting.[12] Hayes was also a therapeutic moderate who prescribed rest and pure air.

Not all of Kirtland's teaching focused on tuberculosis. His surviving lecture notes present a broad review of then-current knowledge of what today is termed internal medicine. A lecture titled "History of the Epidemic Constitution in North America from 1620 to 1856" focused principally on typhus and typhoid. Moreover, his teaching went beyond the narrow confines of modern internal medicine. Volume twenty-three of

his notes contains lectures on neurological diseases, including ones titled: "Apoplexy," "Nervous Irritation of the Brain," "Vascular Irritation
of the Brain," "Passive Congestion of the Brain," "Epilepsy," "Catalepsy,"
"Spinal Irritation," "Spinal Meningitis and Myelitis," and "Chorea."
These topics comprise much of what was understood of neurological diseases at the time.

Kirtland's lecture notes on apoplexy—then the common term for
stroke—reveal a sophisticated understanding of this disease.[13] He distinguished between "congestive" and "sanguineous" attacks, noting that
the latter carried a graver prognosis. This distinction must have been
based on knowledge of autopsy findings. Commenting on the prognosis for patients with apoplexy he noted:

Deep coma with convulsions & general paralysis & uncon-
sciousness continuing one or two days without signs of improvement apt to end fatally.

With respect to treatment he taught:

The usual panacea for Apoplexy—Bloodletting[—]has perhaps
killed as many patients as the disease itself (Killed Walter Scott).

Gastrointestinal disease was common in the nineteenth century.
Sanitation was primitive. Food and water were often contaminated with
disease-causing microbes. In an 1852 letter to C. Smith, MD, Kirtland
provided advice on what was probably chronic diarrhea.[14] One cannot
infer the cause of the illness from the letter, and Kirtland's recommendations were directed more at relief of symptoms than cure.

It is obvious from the result of the course you have lately pursued that your digestive system has been so much impaired
that it is hardly capable of assimilating the necessary amount
of food to sustain health and life.
  Medication may aid under such circumstances but will
never of itself perform a cure.
  Permit me to say that the true mode of restoring that system is to impose upon it no more duty than you can possibly
avoid and to allow it all the time it needs to effect its labors,

and the same time taking equal care not to irritate it with un-congenial food.

Kirtland continued by making specific recommendations for foods at each meal. He prescribed only two meals per day, and his dietary recommendations focused on bland foods, prominently including "mush made out of unbolted wheat flour.... At dinner the mush should supply the place of bread. A little beef steak or fresh meat may be taken." Consistent, perhaps, with medical orthodoxy of the time, Kirtland recommended the use of leeches in an 1851 letter to another physician.

1st indication requires the application early of leeches to tender spots of the abdomen, perineum and verge of the anus. Cupping and scarification may answer but not as serviceable.[15]

This recommendation is surprising, for it was at variance with his generally conservative and palliative recommendations.

In a letter to Mary Ann Riddle, Kirtland offered medical advice concerning her daughter's gastrointestinal illness.

I do not know that I can add many new suggestions in regard to your daughter's case. I suppose it is without doubt a chronic inflammation of the membrane of the stomach. Everything which will irritate or disturb that organ must be avoided. Low and mild diet are essential.[16]

These recommendations reflect the broad sweep of Kirtland's medical expertise. He clearly considered himself an expert in gastrointestinal disease. Indeed, diarrheal disease was common in this era before water purification, and every physician needed to deal with it. Typical of his practice, Kirtland's recommendations were for moderation. Bland diets were the norm in the treatment of most gastrointestinal disease. Only in recent decades has an emphasis on dietary fiber emerged.

Among the most villainous of waterborne diarrheal diseases is cholera. Mortality from it is extremely high. Cholera was present in North America in Kirtland's time, causing epidemics lasting many months and even years. The bacterial cause of cholera was identified by Robert Koch in 1884. Prior to the work of Koch, many individuals with severe diarrhea of other causes were given a diagnosis of cholera. In reading of cholera in the nineteenth century one must realize that other epidemics of diarrheal illness were often called cholera. Kirtland wrote of the disease in an 1851 letter to Dr. John Andrews.

With the approach of the cholera some 3 years since, dysentery has become common and has proved unusually fatal. The result of several cases here led my colleagues ... to engage in a series of post-mortem examinations. They showed that the usual evidence of inflammation existed in the mucous coats of the large intestines and also frequently extended high up into the small ones....

The indications of cure then evidently are -
1st. To subdue inflammation.
2nd. To allay irritation and to take special care not to increase it by our remedies.[17]

In this letter we find Professor Kirtland returning to the theme of his introductory lecture on avoiding harm in prescribing treatment.

Kirtland recognized that a large number of illnesses were transmitted by unsanitary drinking water. He believed that typhoid was among them. He was pioneering in his views; not until 1910 would the United States Public Health Service begin its investigations of safe drinking water from inland rivers. Clevelanders were concerned about their wells, however, and in 1851 the mayor appointed a committee of four local citizens to address the problem of safe water for the city. The committee recommended establishing a system that drew water from Lake Erie. Kirtland took the lead in this effort and devoted his energies to ensuring public acceptance. The facilities for collecting and purifying water from the lake were completed in 1856.

Kirtland received many letters asking for medical advice. Generous with comments to other physicians and to relatives and friends, he was cautious about giving medical advice to those he did not know. In refusing to reply to an inquiry from a Mrs. Mary Malcolm he wrote, "I am so beset, and often insidiously, to give countenance to various kinds of quackery that I am compelled to be very wary of giving opinions lest they should be perverted to improper uses."[18]

Jared Potter Kirtland thought professors who taught subject material relating to medical illness should also practice medicine. He expressed this view strongly to his colleagues J. Lang Cassels and John Delamater in letters written in July 1856. The events that precipitated his communications are unknown. One can infer that they related to the proposed appointment or promotion of Jacob Delamater, John Delamater's son, to the faculty. Kirtland wrote to Cassels:

> There is one point which should be definitely understood and settled among our faculty, "to wit", that no one shall be allowed to occupy a practical chair who is not a regular practitioner in that department. I, for one, will protest against any member who assumes any such chair and fails to bona fidely [sic] engage in its practice and no power shall reign among us so long as any such evasion exists. At the next faculty meeting I shall introduce a resolution to that effect.[19]

There survives a draft resolution among Kirtland's letters and papers that is probably one he drafted as he proposed in his letter to Cassels. It is not evident whether this resolution was presented.

> <u>RESOLVED</u>
>   That no individual shall be deemed competent to fill either of the three practical chairs in the Cleveland Medical College, to wit, <u>Surgery, Theory and Practice of Medicine </u>and <u>Obstetrics</u>, who does not regularly and perseveringly open an office and practice in the department which he professes to fill. Any evasion or failure to comply with the above requisite shall be deemed cause to vacate either of said chairs of their incumbent.[20]

The opening sentences of a Kirtland letter to John Delamater shed some light upon the circumstances that provoked his outbursts.

> There is one point connected with the proposals of Prof. Jacob Delamater to take one of the practical chairs in our institution which should be definitely understood and settled, before the arrangements shall be considered as completed, "to

wit", <u>That he pledges himself to open and continue an office and engage in the practice of the department which he assumes, otherwise the chair is to be deemed as vacated.</u>[21]

In his history of the Western Reserve University School of Medicine, Frederick Waite indicated that little information existed about the younger Delamater and his qualifications.[22] According to Waite, Delamater entered practice with his father in 1844 and was appointed as a lecturer in anatomy and physiology at that time. In 1856 he assumed a professorship of materia medica, therapeutics, and medical jurisprudence. Kirtland's letters presumably related to this appointment.

Kirtland and his colleagues John Delamater and Horace Ackley remained active medical practitioners. They held the first of what became regular clinics at the College of Medicine on November 17, 1847. Ackley treated a broken arm, leg ulcers, and an abscess.[23] On January 5, 1850, the Cleveland *Daily True Democrat* reported on cases seen in their clinic in December 1849 and January 1850.[24] Four patients were seen on the day after Christmas. One week later eleven patients were treated. The diagnoses included a broken collarbone, an infected finger, two leg abscesses, two children with tonsillitis, and a young man with pleurisy. The newspapers continued to report on these clinics. A wide range of conditions were treated, many of them common and minor. Others were more complex, including a case of leprosy, one of syphilis, and surgical repair of a hare lip.

A group of thirteen Cleveland physicians, including Kirtland, established and published a fee schedule for some two dozen therapeutic interventions.[25] Office visits were to be charged for at the rate of $1.00; at night this fee increased to $1.50 to $2.00. (See Table 8.1.) This "Table of Fees," the notice states, "has been, in fact, practically in use for a few years by the Faculty of Cleveland." Indigent patients were treated at no charge by Kirtland and his colleagues at the College of Medicine.

In 1821 the Ohio legislature enacted a law regulating the practice of medicine in the state. Three years later, on February 26, 1824, the legislature repealed that law and passed an act providing for the establishment of medical societies in Ohio.[26] The act created twenty districts for

Amputation of Toes and Fingers	$5.00 to 10.00
Reduction of Dislocation	10.00 to 50.00
Reduction of Hernia	5.00 to 15.00
Dressing of recent Wounds, opening Abscesses...	1.00 to 10.00
Passing of Catheter or Bougie	1.00 to 5.00
Case of Gonorrhea or Syphilis	5.00 to 10.00

Table 8.1. Examples of fees charged for medical treatments in Cleveland by Jared Potter Kirtland and other physicians.

local societies that would be governed by "rules and regulations" prescribed by a state-level General Medical Society. The nineteenth district comprised Cuyahoga and Medina Counties. Prominent local physicians were designated as founders of local societies.

Kirtland, at that time practicing in Trumbull County (in the eighteenth district), was not among the physicians listed in the act. His role in drafting this legislation is not recorded, but it seems unlikely that he had one. Kirtland did, however, keep a copy of the 1824 legislative act authorizing the formation of medical societies in his personal library.

The newly created General Medical Society of the State of Ohio first met on January 5, 1829. Seventeen members were present, none representing the nineteenth district. Subsequent early meetings are not well documented. Annual meetings began in 1835.[27] In 1839 the society met in Cleveland with Kirtland presiding. He presented a paper on malaria at that meeting.

In May 1846 the society was reorganized at a meeting held at the Neil House hotel in Columbus. The present Ohio State Medical Association dates its genesis to that meeting. Kirtland presented a paper on the "Influence of the Diathesis or Epidemic Constitution on the Character of Diseases." In 1848 Kirtland was elected the third president of the association. At a Columbus meeting in 1851 Kirtland reported on the use of opium for the treatment of typhus. The Ohio society returned to Cleveland in 1852 and was reorganized once again at that meeting, with Horace Ackley, Kirtland's medical faculty colleague, now as president.[28]

On May 24, 1824, a group of physicians practicing in the Cleveland area met together and organized the Nineteenth District Medical Society. They elected Dr. David Long president. Long was the first doctor in Cleveland, establishing his practice in 1810 when there were only fifty-seven residents in the community.[29] In April 1840 the medical society elected Kirtland as its president.

Following the Civil War, a Cleveland Academy of Medicine was formed in 1867. It and another local medical society merged to form the Cleveland Medical Association, which reorganized as the Cuyahoga County Medical Society in 1872. Meetings were held sporadically during the ensuing decades, and Kirtland was not further involved with these groups. Not until 1902 was the present Academy of Medicine of Cleveland and Northern Ohio formed. Thus, Kirtland's active role in state-level organized medicine had only a minor local counterpart.

Professor, eminent physician. These appellations easily describe Kirtland today. What, one must ask, did his medical contemporaries think of him? That his students regarded him highly as a lecturer was manifested when they published one of his introductory lectures. John S. Newberry graduated from Western Reserve College in Hudson, Ohio, in 1846. Two years later he earned his MD degree from the Medical College in Cleveland. There he came to know Kirtland, and was soon following him on natural history explorations. Newberry never practiced medicine, but instead devoted his life to the world of nature, especially that of geology, his major interest. He was a founding member of the Geological Society of America, which later evolved into the American Association for the Advancement of Science, and of the National Academy of Sciences. A lifelong friend, he eulogized Kirtland thusly:

> The peculiar personal magnetism of the man was shown not only in the interest which he inspired in the subjects he taught to his medical classes in Cleveland and Cincinnati, but also in the fascination he exerted upon the youth of both sexes who came within the magic circle that surrounded him. In every medical class there were always some, and often many who became his private pupils.
>
> He made flowers bloom and fruits to ripen all along his path in life.[30]

9

Rockport

" [I] was ... so fortunate as to procure 83 acres ... well situated.... As this is one of the finest localities for fruits our country affords I have again directed my attention to their cultivation ... and have procured a great number of the most choice varieties."[1] Thus Jared Potter Kirtland described his purchase of a plot of land in Rockport, Ohio (now Lakewood). The property fronted Detroit Avenue and extended to Lake Erie.

At the time he wrote the words quoted above, Kirtland was living in a house that he owned on St. Clair Street in central Cleveland. He had purchased it after he moved to the city; the 1840 census found him there in Ward 2. He sold his home in Poland to a local farmer named Chauncy Rice. His orchards he left in the care of his brother. The date of this move is somewhat in doubt. All who have written of Kirtland have put it in 1837. Indeed, in a memoir he dictated at age 81, he stated that in August 1837 he "sold his farm in Poland, dissolved his partnership with Dr. Mygatt, and removed to the City of Cleveland where his only child, Mrs. [Mary Elizabeth Kirtland] Pease, and her husband resided."[2]

Kirtland maintained a lively correspondence with Dr. Samuel P. Hildreth of Marietta, Ohio, writing to him every few months. In September 1837 he wrote to him from Poland and talked of an upcoming trip east, from which he expected to be "at home on or about the 23rd of Oct."[3] If he had negotiated the sale of his house and farm in Poland, either he had not yet relinquished title to them or he was at the home of one of his relatives in Poland. Medical school classes in Cincinnati started in November 1837, and Kirtland was obligated to begin his lectures then. One must wonder if he would have had time to negotiate the sale of his farm that autumn. In a letter from Cleveland clearly dated

June 18, 1839, he wrote, "Among the sudden events in the changeable world was the selling of my farm and house in Poland and the purchase of a residence in this city [Cleveland].... I have been here for the last two weeks engaged in purchasing a house and preparing for removing which I expect to accomplish in about six weeks."[4]

Rockport emerged as a village a few miles west of Cleveland early in the nineteenth century. The first cabin was built in 1816 by Charles Mills. Kirtland purchased his farm there in 1840; it would be his residence for the rest of his life. At that time the young Rockport boasted a general store, tavern, and pottery. The first available census data are from 1885, when 400 inhabitants were recorded. A plank road, constructed by laying wood planks across the dirt—and often mud—road surface, connected Rockport to Cleveland. Roads of this type were common in the Western Reserve, where timber for cutting planks was plentiful. The road was originally a poorly maintained toll road. It was appropriated by the town in 1864, but maintenance remained a problem. Throughout Kirtland's life, Rockport was a small hamlet—a rural site that suited his naturalist passions.

Kirtland proceeded to erect a house that would be his permanent residence at what he called Whippoorwill Farm. Work on the house commenced in 1841. It was ready for occupancy in early 1842. The house was built of locally quarried sandstone. It was located on the north side of what is now Detroit Avenue just west of Bunts Road. Additions were made to it in subsequent years, including extra rooms, bay windows, and a sweeping veranda added by his daughter and her family after Kirtland's death. It was finally demolished to make way for a supermarket.

Kirtland purchased additional land adjacent to his property upon which he later built a house for his daughter and her family. In 1841 he wrote to his friend Samuel Hildreth that his property comprised 113 acres. The Pease family moved from Cleveland to Rockport in 1850. Later they extended the added property to reach the lakeshore.

In 1849 the Cleveland and Pittsburgh Railroad Company appropriated a 60-foot strip of land through Kirtland's property. The railroad offered him compensation of one share of stock in the railroad company, which he refused as inadequate. Ultimately a court-appointed appraiser ruled that the benefit to Kirtland of having the rail line in proximity to his residence outweighed the cost of any damages.

In 1867 Kirtland developed a quarry on his land and made improvements to his waterfront. He described these in a letter to his Connecticut cousin Eliza (Lizzie) Potter.

> We have just opened a fine stone quarry near the Lake and find it to yield the best quality of flaggings for city side walks as well as ordinary building purposes.
> To aid in these improvements I have just built a convenient boat and bathing house on the perpendicular bank of the Lake 60 feet above the water and have cut and blasted in the rocky & shaley bank a graded way down to the water, on which is constructed a railway and convenient flight of stairs. Adjacent we have cleared out the forest and formed a beautiful park. Combined these form a pleasant and romantic retreat, and one of the boldest and most picturesque landscapes Ohio affords. It is expected Cleaveland [sic] will establish a park of 250 acres on the right bank of Rocky River.[5]

Kirtland much loved his farm, and he would spend the rest of his days there. "Italy," he wrote, "with its boasted skies cannot excel the view of a summer sunset on Lake Erie."[6]

On March 25, 1842, Kirtland advertised his Cleveland house for rent.

> For Rent - A convenient two-story Brick House, with a small garden, barn, carriage, wood, and coal houses; the place now occupied by myself, and immediate possession will be given to a small family. J. P. Kirtland, St. Clair St.[7]

From his youth with his grandfather Kirtland had found satisfaction not only in cultivating plants but also in developing new varieties, especially of fruits. He had continued this interest in Poland, and looked forward to expanding it in Rockport. As previously noted, he considered the region to be particularly suited for fruit orchards. Fruit trees became the focus of much of his effort. He developed new varieties of pears, apples, and especially cherries, of which he produced more than two dozen new varieties. His correspondence is studded with references to the products of his orchards. In a letter he wrote in 1853 to a Mr. Ellwanger, he extolled his cherry varieties.

> The season is at hand for cutting grafts. Have we anything here which would interest you? If so, inclosed is a list of my seedling cherries. Some of them have been described, others have not, yet not one in the list but has been very thoroughly tested here and I feel certain all will bear the most thorough scrutiny.[8]

There follows a list of seventeen varieties of cherries, "raised from seeds of the Yellow-Spanish ... hybridized by the Black Tartarian, May Duke and Black Mazzards." Kirtland then added a P.S. "N.B. I challenge the horticultural world to produce seventeen varieties (old or new) that will surpass these. This looks like vain boasting - but I make the challenge. J.P.K."[9] Ellwanger's nursery in Rochester, New York, was the largest in North America at that time. It sold Kirtland's cherries in Europe under Kirtland's name.

In the same year he sent grafts of twenty-two cherry varieties to the Massachusetts Horticultural Society. In his cover letter he noted, "Thirty years since I discovered that while the pits of most of the fine varieties of the cherry were abortive, those of the Yellow-Spanish were prolific. Endless new varieties may be produced from them."[10]

Kirtland served as president of the Cleveland Horticulture Society. The society held its evening meetings in his medical school office. He was a regular contributor to its journal, the *Western Reserve Magazine of Agriculture and Horticulture*. His library contained twelve monthly issues published from March 1845 to February 1846; publication probably ceased thereafter. The topics on which he wrote embraced many aspects of horticulture. He commented on peat, noting that extensive beds were to be found in the western parts of the Western Reserve. Based on his experience in Connecticut, he recommended adding barnyard manure, ashes, and lime to garden soil. While guano had "greatly excited of late" the agricultural world, he noted that "every farmer has about his premises a supply of ingredient which if properly saved and compounded would afford an article which if not as stimulating to vegetation as Guano, would be as valuable and far more manageable in most hands."[11]

Kirtland's communications to this horticulture journal reveal the depth of his knowledge and expertise in agriculture. He wrote short essays on farming utensils and on insects "injurious to vegetation." His piece on insects was illustrated with detailed drawings of five species of *Clytus* beetles. He wrote an essay on the history of the tomato as a food. He lamented the use of suckers from diseased trees as stock for new fruit trees. He gave directions for the successful transplanting of tree seedlings. A number of varieties of fruit trees claimed his attention and pen.

Kirtland gave an address to the Oberlin Agricultural and Horticultural Society in 1845. It is a remarkable and insightful analysis of horticultural knowledge gained by art—by which Kirtland meant personal experience—and science. He posed his discussion as a dialogue between the two. While not disputing the value of art/experience, he argued strongly for the more widespread acceptance of agricultural science. He concluded by calling for greater educational opportunities for young people, men and women, heading for agricultural careers.

If Science is destined to fulfill so prominent a part in the pursuit of Agriculture, it becomes an important query— How can the Farming Community best avail themselves of its aid?
The first step towards accomplishing the purpose is to raise the Standard of Education, and extend it universally.[12]

The terrain of northern Ohio was formed by advancing and retreating glaciers. Indeed, these massive sheets of ice carved out Lake Erie. South of the lake, a series of ridges run east-west, once the shores of early glacier-fed lakes. Kirtland knew of this geological history, although not in as much detail as is now understood.

The dry gravelly ridges running parallel to and near the south shore of Lake Erie ... now elevated from one to two hundred feet above the present surface of the Lake are supposed by some of our Geologists once to have been the shore to this fresh water sea.
So far as my observation extends these latter ridges, and especially the one called, from its position, the north ridge, are more favorable for the formation of blow-buds, and at the same time more exempt from the operations of all contingen-

cies unfavorable to the production of fruit, than any locations besides, in the United States.[13]

Orchards in this region produce fruit crops, especially apples, grapes, and peaches, in abundance to the present time. Winter is not always kind to fruit trees in northern Ohio, despite the frost-ameliorating effects of Lake Erie. Damage to fruit buds, Kirtland noted, "is the result of unusually mild and warm weather, suddenly followed by severe cold." However, he noted, orchards close to the lake and on the higher ridges often escaped winter damage for reasons he considered "not very apparent."

Kirtland's knowledge of agriculture was widely recognized by his fellow arborists and farmers in Ohio. In 1845 he attended a convention of farmers in Columbus, Ohio, and at that time was named as one of nine members of the newly organized state board of agriculture. He exhibited regularly at county fairs. In 1860 he displayed a collection of 138 varieties of apples at the Cuyahoga County State Fair.[14]

Productive orchards require bees to pollinate the fruit blossoms. As a boy, Kirtland tended his grandfather's hives. Now in Rockport, he kept bees. A note in the *Cleveland Leader* in January 1859, a time of year when the weather might have interdicted thievery, described the theft of his bees.

For some time in the past there has been a series of thefts and burglaries in Ohio City and the suburbs. A few nights ago, somebody entered the garden of Professor Kirtland, Lake rd., and robbed him of several hives of bees and a quantity of honey.... There is no doubt but what there is a regular gang of thieves who are prowling around with evil intent and who should be placed in "durance vile" for the benefit of the state.[15]

In March of the following year, Kirtland and his fellow beekeepers met to form an association of kindred apiarists. On February 1, 1861, he delivered a lecture on "The Life and Habit of Bees." He recounted ways in which beekeepers may protect themselves, including using a piece of smoking cotton cloth to cause the bees to retreat. He concluded by noting that beekeeping is a pleasant employment for aging and infirm people (Kirtland was sixty-seven at the time, not an advanced age today, but beyond the life expectancy of many men in the nineteenth century).[16]

Beehives were not the only item stolen from Kirtland. He kept a boat on the Rocky River, and in 1856 it was stolen. It was recovered in Cleveland, and at least one of the culprits identified. Kirtland wrote to the father of the youth.

My boat was stolen from Rocky River some days since and brought down to Cleveland. I put the police on the track of the depredators and very conclusive evidence has been obtained that your son, Martin Morgan, was one of the persons engaged in the transaction. The police are only waiting my orders to make arrests.

I learn that you are an industrious and well disposed man who would not uphold such conduct in your son. I therefore take this opportunity to say to you that the affair can be now settled without much trouble but if not promptly attended to, it must take the course of the law.

The value of the boat makes the theft a penitentiary offense. If an arrest is made, the prosecution must go on and with the evidence already obtained must end in a conviction. I trust therefore that you will see to the matter without delay.[17]

Kirtland's surviving correspondence does not provide information about the resolution of this affair. Although he was a liberal and tolerant man, Kirtland was not disposed to ignore or forgive the crime committed against him.

Kirtland entertained many visitors at Whippoorwill Farm. Some were long-standing friends. Others were distinguished scientists in their own right who sought him out because of his professional reputation. Sir

Charles Lyell was an eminent English naturalist and a friend of Charles Darwin. He is said to be the father of the science of geology, having written one of the first major texts on this subject. In June 1842 he visited Kirtland in Cleveland. Kirtland took him to his recently completed home on his lakefront land in Rockport.

> The morning after my arrival at Cleveland, Dr. Kirtland ...
> took me to Rockport, about four miles to the west, and afterwards to the ravine of a torrent called Rocky River.[18]

Kirtland also welcomed eminent French geologist and paleontologist Édouard de Verneuil to his farm.

In January 1855 Lady Anne Murray, Duchess of Athol and Mistress of the Robes to Queen Victoria as well as one of the Queen's closest friends, visited Kirtland. She was in her own right an accomplished naturalist. An egalitarian at heart, Kirtland was awed by the prospect of entertaining an English duchess. However, he "found Miss Murray a plain, well bred lady, of fine scientific attainments and treated her as such. The result was she was pleased far more than any attempts at parade."[19]

Though Kirtland divided his attention between medicine, natural history, and horticulture, he also found room for other interests. One might suppose that living on a farm six miles west of the center of Cleveland represented a retreat from the affairs that might have surrounded him in a more urban setting. In fact, he was very much involved both in Cleveland and his local community. Saddling his horse, he made the trip into the city to lecture at the medical school during its November through February term. He regularly attended meetings of the Arkites in central Cleveland. In 1842 he served as president of a "home league" committee meeting at the Cleveland courthouse to propose bylaws for the city's governance.[20]

Kirtland had an interest in his genealogy, and he spent some time and effort exploring his antecedents. On January 1, 1868, "in the midst of the hilarity and confusion of New Years" he put pen to paper and wrote to his cousin Lizzie Potter.

For several days I have been engaged at the Young Mens Library in arranging and copying the Genealogy of the Kirtland Family from the original Nathaniel K at Lynn, Mass, more than two hundred years since. This pursuit too has awakened the same train of serious thoughts and reflections. Death has closed the scene with every one named in the long and numerous list as far as it has been published....

These genealogical investigations have not only enlarged greatly my circle of acquaintance but my attachment and affection for my hitherto unknown relatives.[21]

The archives of the Mahoning Valley Historical Society contain handwritten notes in a hand other than that of Kirtland labeled, "Extracts from the series of the New England Genealogic and Antiquarian Register, contained in the Cleveland Library, of all that relates to said family made Aug 15, 1871. By Jared Potter Kirtland."[22] Evidently an unknown individual copied Kirtland's notes of 1871 at some later date. These notes would seem to indicate that Kirtland carried his study beyond his local library to the Cleveland Library. The notes contain a fairly complete record of Kirtland's ancestry from the arrival of the Kyrtland brothers in Massachusetts on the *Hopewell*.

Kirtland dictated a personal memoir when he was 81 years old.[23] It comprises 28 closely spaced, typewritten pages. To whom it was dictated and who later transcribed it into a typed document are not known. It contains detailed accounts of his travels that attest to its authenticity. Considered against other evidence of his interest in his family genealogy, it was presumably intended by Kirtland to secure his own place in the family record for future generations,

Kirtland had liberal political views, and was always ready to express them and to become involved with civic-minded, liberal groups. A contemporary newspaper account describes some of these activities.

At an adjourned meeting of the citizens of Cleveland held at the courthouse on Feb 12 for the purpose of carrying out their views in regard to a home league, the committee appointed to report a constitution and officers for their future government reported the following officers: J. Kirtland, M.D., president....[24]

Kirtland was an abolitionist. Slavery was anathema to him. In later newspaper clippings it has been speculated that Kirtland's Rockport farm was a station on the Underground Railroad, perhaps an embarkation point for the crossing of Lake Erie to Canada. There is no confirmable evidence in this regard, but it is not unlikely. As noted in Chapter 5, Kirtland's earlier dwelling in Poland did shelter fugitive slaves.

During the middle years of the nineteenth century in the run-up to the Civil War, political alignments sharpened in the United States. At the founding of the nation, liberals had responded to the leadership of Thomas Jefferson and conservative Federalists had aligned themselves with John Adams. These ideological groupings did not result in the formation of political parties as we know them today, however. As the middle of the nineteenth century dawned, a group known as Whigs emerged. They aligned themselves with small businesses and farms, most notably in the North, but did not identify themselves with slavery-related issues. Free Soil Democrats split from the Whigs and opposed slavery. In June 1848 Kirtland presided over a large meeting of Cleveland citizens who adopted a resolution calling for a national convention to nominate a president favoring "free territory, free soil, and free labor."[25]

Kirtland commented on the Whigs in an 1851 letter.

Ohio has gone Loco-Foco universally. The Whig party here had gradually gained strength till the nomination of Gen. Taylor struck off at one blow about 1/4 of the party. The passage of the fugitive law and the zeal of Fillmore's administration to carry it out, especially in making the Christiana and Syracuse High Treason have paralyzed the other three-quarters. Thousands of men who were staunch Whigs voted the Democratic ticket. Very many stayed at home and others supported the Free Soil nominations.

You may rely upon it that the course of Messrs. Fillmore and Webster, right or wrong, has annihilated the Whig party in Ohio.[26]

In an 1855 letter to a relative living in the South whom he addressed simply as "Respected Relative," Kirtland expressed himself with ardor.

> In regard to slavery I would say that the whole system is wrong.... Mrs. Stowe's work was only fiction based on fact. The spirit of the age will not long endure the cruelties, wrongs and abuses the African race is now enduring at the hands of the American people. They're rendering the Declaration of Independence a farce and our pretensions to freedom and justice ridiculous.[27]

In 1854 Congress passed the Kansas-Nebraska Act, an action that aroused the ire of Kirtland and other abolitionists and liberal thinkers. Under the Missouri Compromise of 1820, slavery had been prohibited in the Nebraska territory. Championed by Illinois senator Stephen Douglas, the Kansas-Nebraska Act set aside portions of the Missouri Compromise and opened Nebraska to slavery. Kirtland and other Northern liberals were much distressed by this action.

Obviously concerned about the future, and perhaps anticipating the Civil War, Kirtland wrote to a fellow physician who may have been a relative of his wife about Northern sentiments concerning slavery. These remarks, of course, may reflect primarily his own liberal views, but he avers that his own sentiments are in accord with those of most of his neighbors.

> The Nebraska matter has aroused a deeper and more unanimous feeling in the North than I supposed any subject could produce.... Since the passage of the Nebraska bill the value of the union among northern people has depreciated as much as some of the fancy stocks among brokers.... Everybody seems to have become stockholders in the "Under Ground Rail Road." Trains are daily passing from the South to the land of freedom....
>
> Last season while pursuing my researches in natural history, I visited upper Canada and spent a Sabbath in visiting the residences of many of the fugitives. I found them in a far better condition than has been represented in the public prints [sic].... Many of them are well off and all are industrious and living comfortably.[28]

In March 1855, Kirtland wrote to Senator S. P. Chase expressing his strong feelings about slavery. Chase had led the opposition to the Kansas-Nebraska Act as it was debated in the Senate. He evoked the specter of the Haitian slave revolt that drove the French from that island and established a nation that copied the American Constitution.

> I saw in Canada many a young Toussant [sic] and Dessalines which such a crisis would develop. It is wise for the South to keep this power unnamed and out of sight but it would be equally wise to dread it being called into operation.[29]

When the Civil War erupted in April 1861 with the Confederate shelling of Fort Sumter, Kirtland was 68 years old and hence unable to join the Union military forces. He volunteered his services to perform physical examinations on recruits for Ohio military units. He donated the pay given to him for this service to the Bounty Fund for Recruits in Rockport and to the Soldiers' Aid Society of Northern Ohio.

Despite all his manifest liberalism and his almost Rousseauian view of African Americans, Kirtland had prejudices. He clearly did not like Catholicism and held those who practiced it in disrespect. He expressed this in a letter to his cousin Sarah Kirtland in Wallingford, Connecticut, writing about a newly hired housekeeper.

> At home all is in confusion. The good English girl, who has lived with us so long, is married this afternoon and we are without help. Mary has started yesterday in pursuit of another. Mrs. K. and her sister, Mrs. Brier, are keeping house with the aid of an Irish girl so overflowing with Romanism that two-thirds of her time she is whispering over Ave Marias in some bye-corner. On Monday we hope to begin the world anew with an intelligent English girl. I hope that Being to whom the Catholics belong will take charge of them for I certainly do not wish them among a Protestant community. The Catholics have had continued preaching and revival in Cleveland for two weeks. That system is a wonderful compound of cunning and iniquity.[30]

Kirtland lived comfortably, but not affluently. Indeed, he was often concerned about his finances. While he may have sold some of his agricultural products, his farm was nonetheless a costly matter. His consultations brought him some income, but not much. He probably would have given up his medical school teaching were it not for the steady income it provided.

Financial concerns had dogged him since his years in Poland. In February 1837 he had written to his friend Samuel Hildreth and declined an invitation to travel with him to Missouri, stating that it was "incompatible with my pecuniary concerns."[31] In September of that year he confided to his friend that he had accepted the teaching appointment in Cincinnati because "the situation of my finances compelled me to take this step."[32] His early financial struggles did not abate with his move to Rockport. In April 1853 he wrote to a Dr. Hubbard about his distress.

I am thinking seriously of removing probably to Shrewsbury, N.J. I am compelled to make some change. My small capital is nearly all invested in bank stock and my farm. On the former I have relied mainly for support but the triple taxation inflicted on banks has absorbed their dividends and I must make some new calculations.[33]

In the pre-antibiotic, pre-immunization, and pre-public health systems era during which Kirtland lived, illness was common. Much of it was caused by microbial pathogens—germs, many waterborne, that we now control or treat readily. Kirtland's correspondence reveals illness frequently dominated life at Whippoorwill Farm

Today we think of malaria as a tropical disease, but it was once widespread in North America. Now it is gone, although the mosquitoes that transmitted it remain a summer nuisance. Kirtland suffered its typical recurring bouts, which he noted in an 1850 letter to his friend Samuel Hildreth.

Malaria has been playing its pranks with me for several years. In September it showed its hand badly and has confined me to my room for 8 weeks & much of that time to the bed. I have now so far recovered as to ride daily into town & deliver lectures at the College.[34]

The imperfect sanitation and lack of safe public drinking water in Ohio at the time made diarrheal illness a common occurrence. In April 1835, Kirtland wrote to Hildreth commenting on his health.

I arrived at home from Columbus with extreme difficulty, after having suffered much from the journey and have been confined to my room and to my bed most of the time since. During the last summer I was attacked with a fever & an obstruction of the liver which terminated with a diarrhoea. The latter symptom continued upon me through the winter.[35]

Cholera also was present and widespread in northern Ohio in the mid-1850s. In February 1850 Kirtland noted that, "An incipient cholera seems to be lurking about us.... I fear the ensuing spring will show it real."[36] Kirtland commented on the spread of cholera in the Midwest to his Connecticut cousin in July 1854.

The cholera is sweeping Chicago and Toledo at this time. Both those places have local causes in abundance to engender it and render it malignant. Cleveland will never be severely scourged with it except in the low streets about the River. At present it is very healthy here.[37]

In fact, Cleveland largely escaped cholera. However, it ravaged Toledo and other Ohio localities, including Rockport, throughout 1853 and into 1854. In August 1854, Kirtland wrote to his sister, "Cholera is on the increase. Families about the mouth of Rocky River are all sick."[38] Kirtland's wife was among those afflicted.

For two days my wife has been greatly reduced by a disease fluctuating between cholera and dysentery. Until this morning it seemed to bid defiance to medication but she is now apparently more comfortable and I think with prudence may recover. There have been some very sudden deaths here and in the vicinity of late, with this form of disease.[39]

That cholera was spread by contaminated drinking water was famously demonstrated by John Snow in London. That happened in 1855, and the news probably did not reached Ohio until after the cholera epidemic had mostly run its course. That a bacterium in water was the cause of cholera would not be demonstrated until 1884 by Robert Koch, the eminent German physician and bacteriologist, who traveled to Egypt and India to study the disease. Even further off were efforts to ensure the safety of American drinking water, which did not take place until the first and second decades of the twentieth century.

Streptococcal (strep) infections we now vanquish quickly with antibiotics. Kirtland had no such recourse. At Christmastime in 1852 he wrote to a niece about an illness characterized by a severe sore throat, which one presumes was caused by streptococci. His account began with a touch of humor.

Like Charity, I will begin at home and first write about myself. For eight weeks I was mostly confined to the house and suffered extremely, more than all other attacks of sickness except dysentery. It was laryngitis and canker like that with which Gen. Washington and Josephine died but that consideration offered no relief from the horrors of suffocation and difficulties of swallowing. I have now so far recovered as to resume my lectures twice each day.[40]

Erysipelas is a rapidly progressing skin infection usually caused by streptococci, and less commonly by staphylococci (staph). Again, Kirtland's letters tell of his experience with this illness. In the summer of 1854 he wrote to an unidentified friend.

Twice since your departure I have commenced writing to you but was ... interrupted by a severe and prolonged attack of erysipelas.... I will not trouble you with details of our domestic sorrows and afflictions. The sum of them is that since last October no day has passed without finding some of my household sick. Scarlet fever and malignant erysipelas has attacked all of our hired help. With the latter I was dangerously sick from the 21st of Feby. till late in April.[41]

The health of Kirtland's daughter and only surviving child, Mary Elizabeth Pease, was frequently a concern. Following the death of her son from congenital heart disease at age 3 on December 17, 1836, she had become severely depressed. From about 1850 on, the Pease family was part of the Kirtland household in Rockport, and Kirtland was close to his surviving grandchildren. Tragedy struck the young Pease family again in 1854 when Frederick Kirtland Pease, their fourth and last child, died on May 22 at age eleven. Kirtland was in Philadelphia at the time, having gone there to visit naturalist colleagues following a meeting of the American Association for the Advancement of Science in Washington, DC. His medical colleague, Horace Ackley, who probably attended the dying child, summoned him home by a telegram. Kirtland attributed the child's death to "erysipelas of the bowels," presumably indicating a diarrheal disease.[42]

Kirtland's wife died on December 23, 1857. There is no evidence of a preceding illness in Kirtland's surviving correspondence. However, there is a ten-year gap in surviving letters beginning in July 1856. Perhaps he was depressed by his wife's illness and death. Having said that, one must also wonder about the relationship between Kirtland and Hannah, his second wife. She bore no children. His letters mention her repeatedly in reference to his health and the health of other members of his household, but seldom in any other context. In reading these letters, one suspects she functioned in his life primarily as a housekeeper, perhaps not as a lover.

Joined by his friends and colleagues from the medical school, Samuel St. John and O. H. Knapp, Kirtland undertook the editing and publication of a semiweekly newspaper, *The Family Visitor*. Usually eight full newspaper pages in size, it was clearly aimed at a family readership. A lead editorial in the first issue on January 3, 1850, defined the proposed scope and editorial direction of the paper.

> Believing that the works of fiction, which occupy so large a
> space in most of the so called family papers of the present
> day, tend to corrupt the heart and debase the mind; that the
> political Press, labors more for the voter, than the family
> circle; and that professedly religious, temperance and literary

papers, from their exclusive character, are circumscribed in their circulation—it will be our object to present a sheet, which ... will be free from those features which limit their circulation, and thus diminish their influence....

In politics, our paper will assume no partizan [sic], and in religion, no bigoted or sectarian character.[43]

True to its stated mission, the editorial content of the paper focused on items of general interest, avoiding all current events and news. Not surprisingly, natural history had a prominent place in its pages. Kirtland republished his accounts of Ohio fishes from his scholarly paper that appeared serially in the *Boston Journal of Natural History* between 1840 and 1847. With them he included meticulous drawings of fish species, identifying each by both common and Linnaean names. Travel articles appeared frequently. News of the medical college was reported regularly. Kirtland solicited contributions from his friends, including Louis Agassiz, the Harvard naturalist. In January 1851 a communication from Reverend B. B. Edwards of Andover, Massachusetts, extolled the virtues of the study of mathematics and classical literature.

In March, after but three months of publication, the paper moved from Cleveland to Hudson, Ohio, and Knapp resigned from its staff. Thereafter *The Family Visitor* continued biweekly for three years.

Kirtland passed many of his Whippoorwill Farm years in Rockport reading works in his extensive personal library. He read Greek and Latin classics in their original languages. His library contained accounts of explorations of the Arctic and other remote areas. In a letter to his cousin Lizzie Potter, he reported,

Baker and wife[’s] journey to the head of the Nile I have just completed. It reads like a novel and is a work of great interest.

Within the last three weeks I have lived over again a life of 73 years in reading the Life of Prof Benjamin Silliman. I have known him well since he returned from Europe in 1805 and he did more to develop a taste for study and scientific research in my early days that all the teachers.[44]

Kirtland's interests included American history, particularly the history of the Western Reserve. In an 1867 paper he considered a number of artifacts that had been found in the sand of the beaches at Rockport.[45] These included such military items as bayonets and fragments of muskets. Kirtland noted that these relics had been found at two principal locations: sandy beaches at the mouth of the Rocky River and a beach known as McMahon's Beach about a mile further west. He sought to identify the origins of these items.

He concluded that they had their origins during Pontiac's War, a three-year conflict that erupted in the wake of the French and Indian War. A British regiment under the command of Major Wilkins embarked in the fall of 1763 to assist the troops at Fort Detroit who were under attack by a group of Native Americans led by Chief Pontiac. On November 7 of that year they were driven ashore by a storm with a loss of twenty boats, 70 men, and three officers. Kirtland quoted from a diary of one of the soldiers garrisoned at Fort Detroit: "This morning two Indians arrived from 'Point-aux-Pins' ... with a letter ... giving an account of the bateaux being cast away, on the 7th instant, at the highlands, beyond said point." Kirtland noted that no locality on the shore of the lake was known as Point-aux-Pins at the time but that an evergreen-covered point jutting into the lake near the Rocky River could have fit the description of a "point aux pines." He concluded that this maritime disaster occurred just east of the mouth of the Rocky River and was responsible for the items found there.

In October 1764, Colonel Bradstreet sailed from Sandusky Bay with 3,000 men aboard a flotilla of bateaux. Contemporary accounts vary with respect to what then ensued. What was clear in Kirtland's view was that the ships were caught in a storm shortly after departing. Twenty-five vessels were lost by being dashed upon the shore. After reviewing historical accounts, Kirtland concluded that this disaster occurred at McMahon's Beach west of the mouth of the Rocky River. Those wrecks produced the artifacts found at that location.

Kirtland's discussion of these two maritime disasters is remarkable for the depth of scholarship he brought to the subject. Although his paper does not include a formal bibliography, it is evident from the text that he consulted many original accounts archived in a variety of sources. As in every aspect of his life, Kirtland displayed the attributes of a scientist and scholar.

As Kirtland's later years evolved, he became less active in the professional and natural history worlds that once consumed him. His health was gradually failing, although the available records do not indicate any specific malady. At some times he was apparently vigorous and active. Recognizing his eminence with respect to the speciation of molluscs, the *American Journal of Conchology* commissioned and published a portrait of him in 1867. It portrays a man in apparent good health. In 1874 he declined an invitation to participate in a bicentennial celebration in Youngstown, Ohio, of which Poland had become a suburb, stating that he was not well enough to make the journey. Yet in 1877 he was well enough to undertake his trip to Florida.

In his later years, Kirtland spent many hours resting in his garden, sitting in a rocking chair with a book in his hands and wearing a warm jacket even on warm, sunny summer days.

As Kirtland approached the end of his life, he recognized that he would soon succumb. He seemed to have accepted approaching death without apprehension. He wrote to Dr. Theodatus Garlick on October 9, 1877.

This is probably my last letter. I am suffering much, and very feeble, but go in peace with my Creator and with all my fellow mortals. Kindest regards to your family circle. Farewell.[46]

He wrote to Garlick again two days later.

Yesterday I was eighty-four years old. A number of friends called, but I was too feeble to see any of them till Mr. Cutter and family called in the afternoon. Too feeble to write more.[47]

He wrote his last letter to Garlick on November 13, 1877.

Every day I grow weaker. My family all attention—kindly watching over me night and day with more anxiety than I feel myself. The great change must soon occur. I have full faith in the Christian hope of a future life, but in what form we are to exist we know not. On the mercies of a kind Providence who created me, who has sustained and helped me through a long life, I rely with a firm faith and hope. We know not what is beyond the grave. Vast multitudes have gone there before us. Love to all. Fare thee well.[48]

Jared Potter Kirtland died at his home on December 10, 1877, at age eighty-four.

Initially buried in a plot on his Whippoorwill Farm, Kirtland's remains were moved in 1883 to Lake View Cemetery in Cleveland where his son-in-law, Charles Pease, had purchased a plot. The remains of other family members were similarly interred there.

At a special meeting of the Kirtland Society shortly after its founder's death, the members adopted a resolution that concluded:

So long as the ocean shall cast a shell upon its shore or fishes populate the American lakes and give food to man, so long as the forest and field shall team [sic] with fauna and flora, the bird of the air build its nest and the bee gather its honey; so long as the tree shall bear its fruit and the vine yield its grape, so long will the people of this land hold in sacred memory the name of Jared Potter Kirtland.[49]

Appendix

Chronology

1635

Nathaniel and Philip Kyrtland emigrated to New England.

1662

King Charles II of England granted to Connecticut the lands between the forty-first and forty-second parallels extending westward to the Pacific Ocean.

November 16, 1755

Turhand Kirtland born in Wallingford, Connecticut.

1786

Competing claims resolved to establish the borders of the Western Reserve of Connecticut.

May 11, 1792

Firelands, comprising 500,000 acres at the western edge of Connecticut's land claim, set aside to compensate residents of Connecticut for damage to their property during the American Revolution.

January 18, 1793

Turhand Kirtland married Mary (Polly) Potter.

November 10, 1793

Jared Potter Kirtland, son of Turhand and Mary Kirtland, born in Wallingford, Connecticut.

September 2, 1795

Connecticut sold the 3 million-acre Western Reserve to the Connecticut Land Company for $1,200,000.

July 22, 1796

Moses Cleaveland and his company of surveyors reached the mouth of the Cuyahoga River.

1797

Jonathan Fowler settled in Poland.

1797

Turhand Kirtland appointed Resident General Agent for the Western Reserve. He moved to Poland, Ohio, the following year.

June 3, 1798

Turhand Kirtland and his party, including surveyor Seth Pease, reached the mouth of the Grand River on Lake Erie and began cutting a road to Poland.

August 29, 1798

Turhand Kirtland reached Poland.

June 17, 1799

David Hudson arrived on his landholding in the Western Reserve, the present site of Hudson, Ohio.

1799

Probable birth year of Jared Potter Kirtland's second wife, Hannah Fitch Toucey.

March 1, 1803

Ohio admitted to the United States as the 17th state.

1803

Turhand Kirtland brought his family to Poland. Jared Potter Kirtland remained in Connecticut with his grandfather, Jared Potter, to finish his education.

1810

Jared Potter Kirtland traveled to Poland, Ohio, where he stayed with his family and taught in the village school.

July 8, 1810

Jared Potter died.

1812

Jared Potter Kirtland began the study of medicine at Yale University. He was the first student to matriculate at the newly organized medical school at Yale.

March 1815

Jared Potter Kirtland received an MD degree from Yale University.

May 22, 1815

Jared Potter Kirtland married Caroline Atwater of Durham, Connecticut.

August 4, 1816

Mary Elizabeth, first child of Jared Potter and Caroline Atwater Kirtland, born in Wallingford, Connecticut.

1818

Jared Potter Kirtland visited Poland, Ohio, with the idea of establishing a medical practice there. He returned to Wallingford and planned to remain in Connecticut.

1818

Jared Potter Kirtland elected to a probate judgeship in Connecticut.

Appendix

September 9, 1818
Jared, second child of Jared Potter and Caroline Atwater Kirtland, born in Wallingford, Connecticut.

1819
René Hyacinthe Théophile Laennec described the stethoscope, which he had invented one year earlier, in a monumental work on tuberculosis. This book was translated into English by John Forbes in 1821.

1819
Jared Potter Kirtland opened his medical practice in Durham, Connecticut.

1819
Ohio Medical College chartered in Cincinnati.

March 27, 1821
Caroline, third child of Jared Potter and Caroline Atwater Kirtland, born in Durham, Connecticut.

September 2, 1822
Caroline, third child of Jared Potter and Caroline Atwater Kirtland, died.

September 18, 1823
Caroline Atwater Kirtland died of "epidemic fever."

1823
Following the death of his wife, Jared Potter Kirtland moved to Poland, Ohio.

March 25, 1824
Jared Potter Kirtland married Hanna Fitch Toucey.

1824
Jared Potter Kirtland established a nursery and orchards in Poland, Ohio, in collaboration with his brothers, Henry and Billius. They established a greenhouse two years later.

1824
Ohio legislature enacted a provision for the establishment of a state and regional medical societies in Ohio.

1826
Jared Potter and Hannah Toucey Kirtland moved into the house built for them in Poland by Turhand Kirtland.

1826
Western Reserve College founded in Hudson by David Hudson.

August 15, 1829
Jared Potter Kirtland, Jr., son of Jared Potter Kirtland and Caroline Atwater Kirtland, died.

1829-1835
Jared Potter Kirtland served three terms in the Ohio legislature.

July 25, 1832
Mary Elizabeth Kirtland married Charles Pease in Boardman, Ohio.

1833
First meeting of the Arkites.

March 3, 1834
Medical College of Willoughby University of Lake Erie chartered by the Ohio Legislature. Classes began on November 3, 1834.

July 1834
Jared Potter Kirtland's seminal paper on the sexual characteristics of molluscs published in the *American Journal of Science and the Arts*.

July 18, 1834
Birth of Jared Potter Kirtland Pease.

1835
The Medical College of Willoughby University of Lake Erie was established.

December 17, 1836
Jared Potter Kirtland Pease, son of Mary Elizabeth and Charles Pease, died of congenital heart disease.

1837
Ohio legislature commissioned a Geological Survey of the State of Ohio.

1837
John Delamater joined the faculty of the Medical College of Willoughby University of Lake Erie.

1837
Jared Potter Kirtland became professor of the theory and practice of physic at the Medical College of Ohio in Cincinnati. During the next four years he spent the winter months in Cincinnati lecturing at the Medical College of Ohio. He returned to Cleveland and, later, Rockport for the rest of the year.

1837
Jared Potter Kirtland purchased a house in Cleveland on St. Clair Street.

1838
The Geological Survey of the State of Ohio was published, including a report on the natural history of the state by Kirtland.

1839
The General Medical Society of Ohio elected Kirtland president.

1840
Jared Potter Kirtland purchased an eighty-three acre farm in Rockport (now Lakewood), Ohio.

1840-1845
Publication of Kirtland's papers on Ohio fishes.

March 1842
Jared Potter Kirtland home at Whippoorwill Farm in Rockport, Ohio, completed.

March 25, 1842

Jared Potter Kirtland advertised his St. Clair Avenue home for rent.

1842

Jared Potter Kirtland resigned from the Medical College of Ohio in Cincinnati and accepted an appointment as professor of theory and practice of physic at the Medical College of Willoughby University of Lake Erie.

November 1, 1842

Jared Potter Kirtland gave the introductory lecture to 70 students at the opening meeting of the 1842-43 session of the Medical College of Willoughby University of Lake Erie.

1843

Jared Potter Kirtland resigned his professorship at the Willoughby Medical College together with John Delamater, Horace Ackley, and John Lang Cassels.

January 3, 1843

Jared Potter Kirtland advertised his expertise as a consultant with special expertise in diseases of the chest.

November 1, 1843

Cleveland Medical College opened with Kirtland delivering the introductory lecture. The other faculty members were John Delamater, Horace A. Ackley, and John Lang Cassels.

February 23, 1844

Ohio legislature amended the charter of Western Reserve College to authorize the establishment of a medical department in Cleveland.

March 20, 1844

Trustees of Western Reserve College adopted the Cleveland Medical College as its Medical Department and awarded diplomas to the men who had finished the course three weeks earlier.

July 23, 1844

First commencement at the Cleveland Medical College with degrees awarded to twenty-five men who had passed an examination.

August 1844

Death of Turhand Kirtland.

1845

Jared Potter Kirtland named to the original board of managers of the Smithsonian Institution.

1845

Jared Potter Kirtland named to the newly organized Ohio State Board of Agriculture.

November 24, 1845

Founding of the Cleveland Academy of Natural Science. Kirtland served as president of the society for 25 years until 1870.

November 4, 1846

Western Reserve College of Medicine opened the first term taught at its newly completed building at the corner of St. Clair Avenue and Erie Street (now East Ninth Street).

1848

Jared Potter Kirtland elected president of the then two-year-old Ohio State Medical Society.

1848

American Association for the Advancement of Science founded. Kirtland was one of the original members.

January 3, 1850

First issue of *The Family Visitor*.

March 24, 1850

Death of Polly Kirtland.

May 1851

American Association for the Advancement of Science met in Cincinnati, Ohio. Kirtland attended and presented his work on the speciation of molluscs.

1851

Discovery of the Kirtland warbler (*Dendroica kirtlandii*).

August 1851

American Association for the Advancement of Science met in Albany, New York. Kirtland attended. He collected specimens on "Coney's Island" after the meeting.

October 10, 1851

Jared Potter Kirtland wrote to Sarah Boardman advising moderation in the treatment of tuberculosis.

1853

Jared Potter Kirtland traveled to Michigan, Ontario, Illinois, and Wisconsin as a member of a natural history survey party.

April 1854

American Association for the Advancement of Science met in Washington, DC. Kirtland attended.

May 27, 1854

Death of Frederick Kirtland Pease, fourth grandchild of Kirtland, at age eleven.

1856

Cleveland opened a water purification system drawing water from Lake Erie.

1856-1857

Jared Potter Kirtland taught that tuberculosis is contagious.

December 23, 1857
Hannah Fitch Toucey Kirtland died in Rockport, Ohio.
1861
Jared Potter Kirtland awarded an honorary LLD by Williams College.
March 3, 1863
National Academy of Sciences chartered.
1864
Jared Potter Kirtland retired and named professor emeritus at age 70.
January 5, 1865
Jared Potter Kirtland elected to membership in the first election of members held by the National Academy of Sciences.
March 1867
Jared Potter Kirtland elected a corresponding member of the Philadelphia Academy of Natural Sciences.
April 1867
Cleveland Academy of Natural Science reorganized with Kirtland as president.
1867
Jared Potter Kirtland resigned from the National Academy of Sciences.
1869
Cleveland Academy of Natural Science renamed the Kirtland Society of Natural Science in honor of Kirtland.
1870
Jared Potter Kirtland traveled to Florida.
January 1875
Jared Potter Kirtland elected to American Philosophical Society.
December 10, 1877
Jared Potter Kirtland died in Rockport, Ohio, at age 84.
September 1882
Western Reserve College moved from Hudson to Cleveland and changed its name to Adelbert College.
1889
City Hospital founded. Its name was changed the following year to Lakeside Hospital.
1910
Flexner report cites Western Reserve College of Medicine for excellence.
1912
Name of the medical school changed to School of Medicine of Western Reserve University.
1920
Cleveland Museum of Natural History founded.

August 18, 1923

Cornerstone laid for a new medical school building on Adelbert Road.

1926

Arkites' natural history collections donated to the Cleveland Museum of Natural History.

Autumn 1928

Ground broken for a new Lakeside Hospital building on Adelbert Road (now University Hospitals Case Medical Center).

1940

Kirtland Society founded at the Cleveland Museum of Natural History, re-organized as the Kirtlandia Society in 1976.

Notes

Chapter 1. Pigs, Flowers, a Horse, and a Bird. Pages 1-4.

1. Mrs. Townsend's Scrapbook. Lakewood History Files. File 7:8. Lakewood Public Library. Transcription deposited in the Kirtland Collection, Special Collections, Kelvin Smith Library, Case Western Reserve University.
2. Ella Grant Wilson, "Dr. Jared P. Kirtland," *Cleveland Plain Dealer* 18 October 1931.
3. Mrs. Townsend's Scrapbook. *Op. cit.*
4. G. Edmund Gifford, Jr., "Doctors Afield: Dr. Jared Kirtland and His Warbler," *New England Journal of Medicine* 287 (1972):909-11.

Chapter 2. Puritan Origins. Pages 5-12.

1. Kirtland, Jared Potter, "Kirtland Family." Copy of handwritten notes. Mahoning Valley Historical Society. Collection 64. Box 17. Files 88.32.15.01.01-88.32.15.01007. "Family Record," Mahoning Valley Historical Society. Collection 64. Box 18. File 88.32.19.08.
2. V. C. Sanford, "The Kirtland or Kirkland Family," In John Ward Dean, ed., *Historical and Genealogical Register. Vol. XLVIII. 1894* (Bowie, MD: Heritage Books, Inc. 1997). Frederick C. Waite, "Jared Potter Kirtland. Physician, Teacher, Horticulturist, and Eminent Naturalist," *Ohio Journal of Science* 30 (1930):153-68. *Vital Records of Saybrook, 1647-1834* (Hartford, CT: The Connecticut Historical Society & the Connecticut Society of the Order of Founders and Patriots of America, 1948). Robert Charles Anderson, *The Great Migration. Immigrants to New England. 1634-1635. Vol. IV* (Boston, MA: New England Historic Genealogical Society, 2005). Charles A. Kirtland, *The Kirtland Family, or, the Descendants of John and Lydia Pratt Kirtland: Who Were Among the First Settlers of Saybrook* (Deep River, CT: Charles A. Kirtland, 1930). I have also consulted several websites, but I have generally relied on published sources.

3. Daniel J. Boorstin, *The Americans. The Colonial Experience* (New York, NY: Vantage Books, 1958).
4. David Hackett Fischer, *Albion's Seed. Four British Folkways in America* (New York, NY: Oxford University Press, 1989). T.H. Breen, *Puritans and Adventurers. Change and Persistence in Early America* (New York, NY: Oxford University Press, 1980).
5. Daniel J. Boorstin, *Op. cit.*
6. T. H. Breen, *Op. cit.*
7. Robert Charles Anderson, *Op. cit.*
8. T. H. Breen, *Op. cit.*
9. *Ibid.*
10. *Ibid.*
11. Harlan Hatcher, *The Western Reserve. The Story of New Connecticut in Ohio* (Indianapolis, IN: The Bobbs-Merrill Company, Inc., 1949).
12. Mary L. W. Morse, "Introduction," In Turhand Kirtland, *Diary of Turhand Kirtland from 1798-1800. While Surveying and Laying out the Western Reserve of the Connecticut Land Company* (Poland, OH: Mary L.W. Morse, 1903).
13. George M. Curtis, "Jared Potter Kirtland, M.D., 'The sage of Rockport,' November 10, 1793-December 18, 1877," *The Ohio State Archaeological and Historical Quarterly* 50 (1941):326-37. Henry H. Fertig, "Some letters of Jared Potter Kirtland," *Ohio State Medical Journal* 51 (1955):553-57.
14. Mahoning Valley Historical Society, *Historical Collections of the Mahoning Valley Containing an Account of the Two Pioneer Reunions: Together with a Selection of Interesting Facts, Traditions, Biographical Sketches, Anecdotes, Etc., Relating to the Sales and Settlement of the Lands Belonging to the Connecticut Land Company and History and Reminiscences, Both General and Local, Vol. I* (Youngstown, OH: Mahoning Valley Historical Society, 1990).
15. Elliot Howard Gilkey, *The Ohio Hundred Year Book. A Hand-Book of the Public Men and Public Institutions of Ohio from the Northwest Territory (1787) to July 1, 1901* (Columbus, OH: Fred J. Heer, 1901). A. B. Coover, "Ohio banking institutions, 1803-1866," *Ohio Archaeological and Historical Publications* 21 (1912):296-320.
16. Mahoning Valley Historical Society, *Op. cit.* This incident is not recounted in Turhand Kirtland's diary as compiled and published in 1903.

Chapter 3. The Western Reserve. Pages 13-24.

1. Harlan Hatcher, *The Western Reserve. The Story of New Connecticut in Ohio* (Indianapolis, IN: The Bobbs-Merrill Company, Inc., 1949). Harry F. Lupold and Gladys Haddad, "Conquest and Settlement: Native Americans to New Englanders," In Lupold, Harry F. and Haddad, Gladys, eds., *Ohio's Western Reserve. A Regional Reader* (Kent, OH: The Kent State University Press,

1988). Thomas E. Ferguson, *Ohio Lands. A Short History. Third Edition* (Columbus, OH: Ohio Auditor of State, 1991). Wheeler, Robert A. "The Connecticut Generis of the Western Reserve," *Ohio History* 114 (2007): 57-78.

2. Benjamin Franklin, "A Plan for Settling Two Western Colonies, 1755," Reproduced in Wheeler, Robert A., ed., *Visions of the Western Reserve. Public and Private Documents of Northeastern Ohio, 1750-1860* (Columbus, OH: Ohio State University Press, 2000).

3. Harlan Hatcher, *Op. cit.*

4. *Ibid.* Hatcher gives a coherent account of these confusing transactions.

5. Samuel P. Orth, "Appendix," *A History of Cleveland Ohio with Numerous Chapters by Special Contributors. Vol. I* (Cleveland, OH: The S.J. Clarke Publishing Co., 1910).

6. *Ibid.* Harvey Rice, *Sketches of Western Reserve Life* (New York, NY: Lee and Shepard, 1888). Harry F. Lupold and Gladys Haddad, *Op. cit.*

7. *History of Trumbull and Mahoning Counties with Illustrations and Biographical Sketches. Vol. I* (Cleveland, OH: H.Z. Williams & Bro. 1882). This publication includes quotations from the journals of survey party members.

8. Russell H. Anderson, "The Pease Map of the Connecticut Western Reserve," *The Ohio State Archaeological and Historical Quarterly* 63 (1954):270-82.

9. Turhand Kirtland, *Diary of Turhand Kirtland from 1798-1800. While Surveying and Laying Out the Western Reserve for the Connecticut Land Company* (Poland, OH: Mary L.W. Morse, 1903). Subsequent quotations from Kirtland's diary are from this source.

10. Samuel P. Orth, *Op cit.*

11. Grace Goulder Izant, *Hudson's Heritage. A Chronicle of the Founding and Flowering of the Village of Hudson, Ohio* (Kent, OH: The Kent State University Press, 1985). George W. Knepper, "Early Migration to the Western Reserve," In Harry F. Lupold and Gladys Haddad, eds, 1988, *Op. cit.*

12. Frederick Clayton Waite, *Western Reserve University. The Hudson Era. A History of Western Reserve College and Academy at Hudson, Ohio, from 1826-1882* (Cleveland, OH: Western Reserve University Press, 1943).

Chapter 4. Connecticut. Pages 25-40.

1. Charles Henry Stanley Davis, *History of Wallingford, Conn. From its Settlement in 1670 to the Present Time, Including Meriden, which was one of its Parishes until 1806, and Cheshire, which was Incorporated in 1780* (Meriden, CT: Published by the Author, 1870). Turhand Kirtland, *Diary of Turhand Kirtland from 1798-1800: While Surveying and Laying Out the Western Reserve for the Connecticut Land Company* (Poland, OH: Mary L.W. Morse, 1903).

2. The most important sources of information about Kirtland's life are: Jared Potter Kirtland, *Biographical Sketch of Dr. Jared Potter Kirtland Probably Dictated by Him at Age 81*. Copy deposited at the Cleveland Museum of Natural History by Margaret Manor Butler. Agnes Robbins Gehr, "Jared Potter Kirtland, 1793-1877." Thesis submitted in partial fulfillment of the requirements for the Degree of Master of Arts, Department of American Culture, Western Reserve University, 1950. A number of published sources also provide information about Jared Potter Kirtland's early life. J. S. Newberry, "Memoir of Jared Potter Kirtland, 1793-1877." Read before the National Academy, April 18, 1879. *National Academy of Sciences: Bibliographical Memoirs: Vol. II* (Washington, DC: The Academy, 1886). This essay is of particular interest because it was written by a man who knew Kirtland during his life. Albert R. Baker and Samuel W. Kelley, "Editorial," *Cleveland Medical Gazette* 6 (1890):3-39. One or both of these writers may also have known Kirtland. Maurice Joblin, *Cleveland, Past and Present: Its Representative Men. Comprising Biographical Sketches of Pioneer Settlers and Prominent Citizens: With a History of the City and Historical Sketches of Its Commerce, Manufactures, Ship Building, Railroads, Telegraphy, Schools, Churches, Etc.* (Cleveland, OH: Fairbanks, Benedict & Co., Printers, 1869). Although brief, this article was also written during Kirtland's lifetime. Frederick C. Waite, "Jared Potter Kirtland—physician, teacher, scientist," *Bulletin of the Cleveland Academy of Medicine* 14, no. 7 (1930):56. Frederick C. Waite, "Jared Potter Kirtland, Physician, Teacher, Horticulturist, and Eminent Naturalist," *The Ohio Journal of Science* 30 (1930):153-68. Frederick C. Waite, "Jared Potter Kirtland: The Sage of Rockport," In Howard Dittrick, ed., *Pioneer Medicine in the Western Reserve* (Cleveland, OH: The Academy of Medicine of Cleveland, 1932). George M. Curtis, "Jared Potter Kirtland, M.D.: Pioneer Naturalist of the Western Reserve: November 10, 1793-December 18, 1877," *Ohio State Medical Journal* 37 (1941):971-77. George M. Curtis, "Jared Potter Kirtland, M.D.: 'The Sage of Rockport:' November 10, 1793-December 18, 1877." *The Ohio State Archeological and Historical Quarterly* 50 (1941):326-37.
3. Charles Henry Stanley Davis, 1870. *Op cit.*
4. *Papers of the New Haven Colony Historical Society, Volume II* (New Haven, CT: Printed for the Society, 1877). Accessed May 4, 2011, http://archive.org/details/papersofnewhavenv2newh
5. *Ibid.*
6. Jared Potter Kirtland to Benjamin I. Lossing, Esq. 5 November 1852. In *Letters Written by Dr. Jared Potter Kirtland February 8, 1850 to June 27, 1853*, transcribed by Harold T. Clark, Archives of the Allen Medical Library, Health Sciences Library, Case Western Reserve University, Cleveland, Ohio.
7. Jared Potter Kirtland to Dear Cousin, 5 December 1852. In *Letters Written by Dr. Jared Potter Kirtland February 8, 1850 to June 27, 1853*, transcribed

by Harold T. Clark, Archives of the Allen Medical Library, Health Sciences Library, Case Western Reserve University, Cleveland, Ohio. The cousin to whom this letter was addressed was Sarah, one of the daughters of Sarah and Billius Kirtland, who moved to the elder Potter's home after the death of her parents.

8. Jared Potter Kirtland to Cousin Sarah, 11 April 1853. In *Letters Written by Dr. Jared Potter Kirtland February 8, 1850 to June 27, 1853*, transcribed by Harold T. Clark, Archives of the Allen Medical Library, Health Sciences Library, Case Western Reserve University, Cleveland, Ohio.

9. Charles Henry Stanley Davis, 1870. *Op. cit.*

10. William B. Sprague, *Annals of the American Pulpit or Commemorative Notices of Distinguished American Clergymen of Various Denominations from the Early Settlement of the Country to the Close of the Year Eighteen Hundred and Fifty-five. Vol. V* (New York, NY: Robert Carter & Brothers, 1861).

11. Frederic C. Waite, *The Ohio Journal of Science* 1930. *Op. cit.*

12. Jared Potter Kirtland, *Biographical Sketch of Dr. Jared Potter Kirtland Probably Dictated by Him an Age 81. Op. cit.*

13. *Ibid.*

14. *Ibid.*

15. George M. Curtis, *Op. cit.* Curtis attributes this quotation to Jared Potter Kirtland. He does not give a source, and I have not been able to find an original letter or other document containing this text.

16. Howard C. Aley, *A Heritage to Share: The Bicentennial History of Youngstown and Mahoning County, Ohio* (Youngstown, OH: The Bicentennial Commission of Youngstown and Mahoning County, Ohio, 1975).

17. Jared Potter Kirtland, *Biographical Sketch of Dr. Jared Potter Kirtland Probably Dictated by Him at Age 81. Op. cit.*

18. Jared Potter Kirtland to Mr. John M. Edwards, 1874. Quoted in Dudley P. Allen, "Pioneer Medicine on the Western Reserve," *Magazine of Western History* 4 (1886):190-99.

19. Jared Potter Kirtland, *Biographical Sketch of Dr. Jared Potter Kirtland Probably Dictated by Him at Age 81. Op. cit.*

20. *Papers of the New Haven Colony Historical Society*, *Op. cit.*

21. William Chauncey Fowler, *History of Durham Connecticut, from the First Grant of Land in 1662 to 1866.* (Hartford, CT: Press of Wiley, Waterman & Eaton, 1866). This volume was in Kirtland's private library and contains pencil marginal notes in his handwriting. Thus, it is probably more accurate than later accounts of Kirtland's education. J. S. Newberry, *Op. cit.*

22. Howard A. Kelley, *A Cyclopedia of American Medical Biography Comprising the Lives of Eminent Deceased Physicians and Surgeons from 1610 to 1910. Vol. II* (Philadelphia, PA: W.B. Saunders Company, 1912).

23. Anson Phelps Stokes, *Memorials of Eminent Yale Men: A Biographical Study of Student Life and University Influences During Eighteenth and Nineteenth Centuries. Vol. II. Science and Public Life* (New Haven, CT: Yale University Press, 1914).

24. J. S. Newberry, *Op. cit.*

25. William Chauncey Fowler, *Op. cit.*

26. Extract of a Letter of Jared Potter Kirtland, LL.D. Published in William Chauncey Fowler, *Op. cit.*

27. William Chauncey Fowler, *Op. cit.*

28. *Ibid.*

29. Jared Potter Kirtland, "Vol. 4: History of the Epidemic Constitution in North America from 1620 to 1856," Handwritten notes for lectures at the Cleveland Medical College archived in the Kelvin Smith Library, Special Collections, Case Western Reserve University, Cleveland, Ohio.

Chapter 5. Poland. Pages 41-54.

1. Jared Potter Kirtland, *Biographical Sketch of Dr. Jared Potter Kirtland Probably Dictated by Him at Age 81.* Copy deposited at the Cleveland Museum of Natural History by Margaret Manor Butler.

2. Rebecca M. Rogers, "Dr. Jared P. Kirtland: Amateur of Horticulture," *Journal of Garden History* 6 (1986):357-75. Ohio State Board of Agriculture, *The Farmers' Centennial History of Ohio 1803-1903* (Springfield, OH: The Springfield Publishing Company, State Printers, 1904). Much additional information was obtained in interviews with historian Rebecca Rogers.

3. Ohio State Board of Agriculture, *Op. cit.*

4. Dudley P. Allen, "Pioneer medicine on the Western Reserve," *Magazine of Western History Illustrated* 4 (1886):444-52. The author states that this article is based upon a conversation with Mygatt a few months before the latter's death.

5. Jared Potter Kirtland, *Biographical Sketch of Dr. Jared Potter Kirtland Probably Dictated by Him at Age 81. Op. cit.*

6. *Ibid.*

7. *Ibid.*

8. Jean Nathan, chairman, *Ohio Marriages Recorded in County Courts: 1 Jan 1821 31 Dec 1830: An Index* (Mansfield, OH: The Ohio Genealogical Society, 2003). Roberta Graves Hyde, Sally Bloomfield Mazer, and Barbara Houser Layfield, eds., *Trumbull County Ohio Marriage Record Index: One Hundred Years: 1800-1900: Volume I, A-M* (Cortland, OH: Howard Printing, 1998). The name Toucey is misspelled in both of these works, probably as a result of copying from handwritten records.

9. Albert R. Baker and Samuel W. Kelley, "Editorial," *Cleveland Medical Gazette* 6 (1890):339. This obituary was almost certainly the source of information for other early biographical pieces, some of which borrowed wording unchanged without attribution.
10. Newtown, "Vital records of Newtown, Connecticut," Undated typescript archived at the Western Reserve Historical Society, Cleveland, Ohio.
11. Rebecca Rogers, email communication dated 14 June 2011.
12. *The Cleveland Plain Dealer* 39 (100) 26 April 1883.
13. Carl Guess, *Ohio House of Representatives Membership Directory: 1803-1965/66* (Columbus, OH: Columbus Blank Book Co., 1966).
14. Jared Potter Kirtland, *Biographical Sketch of Dr. Jared Potter Kirtland Probably Dictated by Him at Age 81. Op. cit.*
15. Jared Potter Kirtland to Dr. Hildreth, 28 February 1837. Archives of the Cleveland Museum of Natural History. Copy deposited by Margaret Maron Butler in 1980.
16. Jared Potter Kirtland, *Biographical Sketch of Dr. Jared Potter Kirtland Probably Dictated by Him at Age 81. Op. cit.*
17. Jared Potter Kirtland to Dr. Hildreth, 28 February 1837. *Op. cit.*
18. James Thomas Flexner, *Doctors on Horseback. Pioneers of American Medicine* (New York: The Viking Press, 1937).
19. *Ibid.*
20. William Chauncey Fowler, *History of Durham Connecticut, from the First Grant of Land in 1662 to 1866* (Hartford, CT: Press of Wiley, Waterman & Eaton, 1866).
21. R. H. Collyer, *Manual of Phrenology or the Physiology of the Human Brain Embracing a Full Description of the Phrenological Organs, their Exact Location, and the Peculiarities of Character Produced by their Various Degrees of Development and Combination* (Cincinnati, OH: Alexander Flash, 1838).
22. Patsy A. Gerstner, "The Personality of Jared Potter Kirtland as Revealed by Phrenology," *Bulletin of the Cleveland Medical Library* 18 (1971):60-63.

Chapter 6. Western Reserve University School of Medicine. Pages 55-68.

1. Hippocrates, *The Aphorisms of Hippocrates*, Trans. Thomas Coar (Birmingham, AL: The Classics of Medicine Library, 1982).
2. Frederick Clayton Waite, *Western Reserve University Centennial History of the School of Medicine* (Cleveland, OH: Western Reserve University Press, 1946).
3. Works Projects Administration in Ohio, *Annals of Cleveland—1818-1935. Volume 20. Abstracts from the Cleveland Herald. January 1 to December 31, 1837, abstract 1143*, 1937.
4. Frederick Clayton Waite, 1946. *Op. cit.*

5. Agnes Robbins Gehr, "Jared Potter Kirtland," *The Explorer* 2, no. 7 (1952): 1-33.
6. Frederick C. Waite, "Medical Education in Ohio," *Ohio State Medical Journal* 49 (1953):623-26.
7. James Harrison Kennedy, *A History of the City of Cleveland, Its Settlement and Progress, 1796-1896* (Cleveland, OH: The Imperial Press, 1896). Frederick C. Waite, *An Historical Sketch of the Willoughby Medical College, 1834-1847* (Cleveland, OH: Western Reserve University, 1934) pamphlet archived at the Allen Medical Library of Case Western Reserve University. Frederick C. Waite, 1946. *Op. cit.* Randolph C. Downes, *History of Lake Shore Ohio* (New York, NY: Lewis Historical Publishing Company, Inc., 1952).
8. Works Projects Administration of Cleveland, *Annals of Cleveland—1818-1935. Vol. 20. Abstracts from the Cleveland Herald, January 1 to December 31, 1837, abstract 1142,* 1937.
9. Frederick C. Waite, "John Delamater, educator and physician, founder of the School of Medicine of Western Reserve University," *Bulletin of the Academy of Medicine of Cleveland* 14, no. 5 (1930):9-10, 18, 20. This same article was published two years later as a chapter in: Howard Dittrick, *Pioneer Medicine in the Western Reserve* (Cleveland, OH: The Academy of Medicine of Cleveland, 1932).
10. Circular and Catalogue of the Offices, Professor and Students of Willoughby University at Willoughby, Lake County, O. Session 1842-43 (Cleveland, OH: T.H. Smead, 1842).
11. Howard Dittrick, "The colorful career of Horace Ackley," In Howard Dittrick, *Pioneer Medicine in the Western Reserve* (Cleveland, OH: The Academy of Medicine of Cleveland, 1932).
12. J. Lang Cassels, "Notice of a meteorite which fell in Hindustan in 1857," *American Journal of Science* 32, no. 96 (1861):51-53.
13. Works Projects Administration in Ohio, *Annals of Cleveland—1818-1935. Vol. 25. Abstracts from the Cleveland Herald, January 1 to December 31, 1842, abstract 1278,* 1937.
14. Frederick C. Waite, 1934. *Op. cit.* Exhuming cadavers from graves for use in dissection was a common practice at that time, usually carried out stealthily by students at night.
15. Grace Goulder Izant, *Hudson's Heritage: A Chronicle of the Founding and Flowering of the Village of Hudson, Ohio* (Kent, OH: The Kent State University Press, 1985).
16. Records of the Trustees of Western Reserve College, Hudson, Ohio from March 1, 1826, to August 28, 1834. Case Western Reserve University Archives, series 2JD, box 1.

17. Frederick Clayton Waite, 1946. *Op. cit.* Frederick Clayton Waite, *Western Reserve University: The Hudson Era: A History of Western Reserve College and Academy at Hudson, Ohio, from 1826-1882* (Cleveland, OH: Western Reserve University Press, 1943). Clarence Henly Cramer, *Case Western Reserve: A History of the University: 18261976* (Boston, MA: Little, Brown and Company, 1976).

18. Hiram Collins Haydn, *Western Reserve University from Hudson to Cleveland 1878-1890: An Historical Sketch* (Cleveland, OH: Western Reserve University, 1905).

19. Works Projects Administration in Ohio, *Annals of Cleveland—1818-1935. Vol. 27. Abstracts from the Cleveland Herald. January 1 to December 31, 1844, abstract 1057, 1937.*

20. Extracts from the Minutes of the Meetings of the Faculty of the Medical Department of Western Reserve University from 1843 to June, 1909. Case Western Reserve University Archives, series 24FJ, box 1, folder 1.

21. *Ibid.*

22. Works Projects Administration in Ohio, *Annals of Cleveland1818-1935. Vol. 26. Abstracts from the Cleveland Herald. January 1 to December 31, 1843, abstract 1211, 1937.*

23. Extracts from the Minutes of the Meetings of the Faculty of the Medical Department of Western Reserve University from 1843 to June, 1909. *Op. cit.* Jared Potter Kirtland to Robt Thompson, M.D. 10 February 1850. In *Letters Written by Dr. Jared Potter Kirtland February 8, 1850 to June 27, 1853,* transcribed by Harold T. Clark. Archives of the Allen Medical Library, Health Sciences Library, Case Western Reserve University, Cleveland, Ohio.

24. Works Projects Administration in Ohio, *Annals of Cleveland—1818-1935. Vol. 29. Abstracts from the Cleveland Herald. January 1 to December 31, 1846, abstracts 951 and 954, 1937.*

25. Frederick C. Waite, 1953. *Op. cit.*

26. Jared Potter Kirtland to W.H. Scoby, M.D., 27 January, 1853. Archives of the Dittrick Medical Center, Case Western Reserve University, Cleveland, Ohio.

27. Works Projects Administration in Ohio, *Annals of Cleveland—1818-1935. Vol. 35. Abstracts from the Daily True Democrat. January 1 to December 31, 1852, abstract 1106, 1937.* See also Frederick C. Waite, 1946. *Op. cit.*

28. Abraham Flexner, *Medical Education in the United States and Canada: A Report to the Carnegie Foundation for the Advancement of Teaching: With an Introduction by Henry S. Pritchett* (New York, NY: Carnegie Foundation for the Advancement of Teaching, 1910).

29. Greer Williams, *Western Reserve's Experiment in Medical Education and Its Outcome* (New York, NY: Oxford University Press, 1980).

Chapter 7. Naturalist. Pages 69-86.

1. Jared Potter Kirtland, *Biographical Sketch of Dr. Jared Potter Kirtland Probably Dictated by Him at Age 81*. Copy deposited in the archives of the Cleveland Museum of Natural History by Margaret Manor Butler.

2. J. S. Newberry, "Memoir of Jared Potter Kirtland, 1793-1877," Read before the National Academy, April 18, 1879, *National Academy of Sciences: Biographical Memoirs*, Vol. 2 (Washington, DC: The Academy, 1886). Albert R. Baker and Samuel W. Kelley, "Editorial. Jared Potter Kirtland," *Cleveland Medical Gazette, A Monthly Journal of Medicine and Surgery* 6 (1891):3-39.

3. Albert R. Baker and Samuel W. Kelley, *Op. cit.*

4. Bernard McMahon, *The American Gardener's Calendar; Adapted to the Climates and Seasons of the United States* (Philadelphia, PA: B. Graves, 1806).

5. Rogers, Rebecca M., "Dr. Jared P. Kirtland: Amateur of Horticulture," *Journal of Garden History* 6 (1986):357-75. This scholarly paper provides extensive information about Kirtland's horticultural activities.

6. *Ibid.*

7. Erik Stokstad, "Nearly Buried, Mussels Get a Helping Hand," *Science* 338 (2012):876-78.

8. Jared Potter Kirtland, "Observations on the Sexual Characters of the Animals Belonging to Lamarck's Family of *Naiades*." *American Journal of Science and Arts* 26 (1834):117-20.

9. Thomas Say, *American Conchology or Descriptions of the Shells of North America: Illustrated by Coloured Figures from Original Drawings Executed from Nature* (New Harmony, IN: School Press, 1830). The copy of this volume from Kirtland's library is now in the closed stacks of the Allen Medical Library, Case Western Reserve University, Cleveland, Ohio.

10. Jared Potter Kirtland, "Observations on the Sexual Characters of the Animals Belonging to Lamarck's Family of *Naiades*." *Op. cit.*

11. *Biographical Sketch of Dr. Jared Potter Kirtland Probably Dictated by Him at Age 81. Op. cit.*

12. Jared Potter Kirtland to S. P. Hildreth, M.D. 4 February 1835. Archives of the Cleveland Museum of Natural History. Copy deposited by Margaret Manor Butler in 1980.

13. William W. Mather, *First Annual Report of the Geological Survey of the State of Ohio* (Columbus, OH: Samuel Medary, Printer to the State, 1838).

14. Constantine S. Rafinesque, *Ichthyologia Ohiensis, or Natural History of the Fishes Inhabiting the River Ohio and its Tributary Streams* (Lexington, KY: W. G. Hunt, 1820).

15. "Dr. Samuel P. Hildreth of Ohio." *The Boston Medical and Surgical Journal* 41 (1849):229-32.

16. Maurice Joblin, *Cleveland Past and Present: Its Representative Men* (Cleveland, OH: Fairbanks, Benedict, 1869).

17. Frederick C. Waite, "Jared Potter Kirtland, Physician, Teacher, Horticulturist, and Eminent Naturalist," *The Ohio Journal of Science* 30 (1950):153-68. In this paper, as in nearly all of his publications, Waite gives no citations, so it is difficult to confirm his statements.

18. Jared Potter Kirtland, "Descriptions of Four New Species of Fishes," *Boston Journal of Natural History* 3 (1840-1841):273-77.

19. Jared Potter Kirtland, "Descriptions of the Fishes of the Ohio River and its Tributaries," *Boston Journal of Natural History* 3 (1840-1841):338-52; 3 (1840-1841):469-82; 4 (1843-1844):15-26; 4 (1843-1844):231-40; 4 (1843-1844):303-8; 5 (1845-1847):21-32; 5 (1845-1847):265-76; 5 (1845-1847):330-34.

20. Jared Potter Kirtland to an unidentified colleague 1851, In *Letters Written by Dr. Jared Potter Kirtland February 8, 1850 to June 27, 1853*, transcribed by Harold T. Clark, Archives of the Allen Medical Library, Health Sciences Library, Case Western Reserve University, Cleveland, Ohio.

21. Jared Potter Kirtland, "Peculiarities of Climate, Flora and Fauna of the South Shore of Lake Erie in the Vicinity of Cleveland, Ohio," *American Journal of Science and the Arts* 13 (1852):215-19. Also, *Proceedings of the Cleveland Academy of Natural Science 1845 to 1859* (Cleveland, Ohio: Published by a Gentleman, 1874).

22. Jared Potter Kirtland, "Peculiarities of Climate, Flora and Fauna of the South Shore of Lake Erie in the Vicinity of Cleveland, Ohio." *Op. cit.*

23. Jared Potter Kirtland to Dr. Hildreth 28 February 1837. Archives of the Cleveland Museum of Natural History. Copy deposited by Margaret Manor Butler in 1980.

24. Jared Potter Kirtland to Rev. J. Bachman 13 November 1851, In *Letters Written by Dr. Jared Potter Kirtland February 8, 1850 to June 27, 1853*, transcribed by Harold T. Clark, Archives of the Allen Medical Library, Health Sciences Library, Case Western Reserve University, Cleveland, Ohio.

25. *Proceedings of the American Association for the Advancement of Science: First Meeting, Held at Philadelphia September, 1848* (Philadelphia, PA: John C. Clark, 1849).

26. *A History of the First Half–Century of the National Academy of Sciences: 1863-1913* (Baltimore, MD: The Lord Baltimore Press, 1913). Rexmond C. Cochrane, *The National Academy of Sciences: The First Hundred Years: 1863-1963* (Washington, DC: National Academy of Sciences, 1978).

27. Jared Potter Kirtland to Dr. Badley 12 January 1852, In *Letters Written by Dr. Jared Potter Kirtland February 8, 1850 to June 27, 1853*, transcribed by Harold T. Clark, Archives of the Allen Medical Library, Health Sciences Library, Case Western Reserve University, Cleveland, Ohio.

28. "Origin of the Society," *Proceedings of the Cleveland Academy of Natural Science: 1845 to 1859* (Cleveland, OH: A Gentleman of Cleveland, 1874).

29. Walter B. Hendrickson, *The Arkites and Other Pioneer Natural History Organizations of Cleveland* (Cleveland, OH: The Press of Western Reserve University, 1962).

30. "Cleveland Academy of Natural Science," *Proceedings of the Cleveland Academy of Natural Science 1845 to 1859* (Cleveland, OH: A Gentleman of Cleveland, 1854). "Memoranda Respecting the Property Contained in the Museum of the Cleveland Academy of Natural Science," *Proceedings of the Cleveland Academy of Natural Science 1845 to 1859* (Cleveland, OH: A Gentleman of Cleveland, 1854).

31. "Origin of the Society." *Op. cit.*

32. Works Projects Administration in Ohio, *Annals of Cleveland—1818-1935. Vol. 29. Abstracts from the Cleveland Herald. January 1 to December 31, 1846.* Abstract 1225, 1937.

33. Jared Potter Kirtland to Prof. Agassiz 25 September 1851, In *Letters Written by Dr. Jared Potter Kirtland February 8, 1850 to June 27, 1853*, transcribed by Harold T. Clark, Archives of the Allen Medical Library, Health Sciences Library, Case Western Reserve University, Cleveland, Ohio. Jared Potter Kirtland to Rev. I. Bachman, Nov 17, 1851, In *Letters Written by Dr. Jared Potter Kirtland February 8, 1850 to June 27, 1853*, transcribed by Harold T. Clark, Archives of the Allen Medical Library, Health Sciences Library, Case Western Reserve University, Cleveland, Ohio.

34. *The Explorer: The Cleveland Museum of Natural History* 2, no. 7 (1952):1.

35. John Bachman to Jared Potter Kirtland, 26 March 1852. Published in *Proceedings of the Cleveland Academy of Natural Science: 1845 to 1859* (Cleveland, OH: A Gentleman of Cleveland, 1874).

36. John Large, Jr., "A Scientist Observes Florida: 1870" *Florida Historical Quarterly* 42 (1963):48-54. *Biographical Memoir of Dr. Jared Potter Kirtland Probably Dictated by Him at Age 81. Op. cit.* Jared Potter Kirtland to Miss Lizzie S. Potter 10 February 1870, Archives of the Cleveland Museum of Natural History. Copy deposited by Margaret Manor Butler in 1980.

37. Jared Potter Kirtland to Miss Lizzie S. Potter 10 February 1870. *Op. cit.*

Chapter 8. Physician, Professor. Pages 87-106

1. Jared P. Kirtland, M.D., *Introductory Lecture on the Coinciding Tendencies of Medicines* (Cleveland, OH: Steam Press of M. C. Younglove & Co., 1848). Kirtland Collection, Kelvin Smith Library Special Collections, Case Western Reserve University, Cleveland, Ohio.

2. Works Projects Administration in Ohio, *Annals of Cleveland—1843-1844. Vol. 26, Abstracts from the Cleveland Herald. January 3, 1843, abstract 1186, 1843.*

3. René T. H. Laennec, *A Treatise on the Disease of the Chest in which they are Described According to their Anatomical Characters, and their Diagnosis Es-*

tablished on a New Principle by Means of Acoustick Instruments. Translated from the French by John Forbes, M.D. (London: T. and G. Underwood, 1821).

4. E. R. N. Grigg, "The arcana of tuberculosis with a brief epidemiologic history of the disease in the U.S.A. Part III. Epidemiologic history of tuberculosis in the United States," *American Review of Tuberculosis and Pulmonary Disease* 78 (1958): 426-53.

5. René T. H. Laennec, *Op. cit.*

6. Charles J. B. Williams, *Op. cit.*

7. Thomas Hayes, *A Serious Address on the Dangerous Consequences of Neglecting Common Coughs and Colds with Ample Directions for the Prevention and Cure of Consumptions to which are Added Observations on the Hooping Cough and Asthma* (Boston, MA: Samuel Etheridge, 1796).

8. Jared Potter Kirtland, Handwritten lecture notes. Kirtland Collection, Kelvin Smith Library Special Collections, Case Western Reserve University, Cleveland, Ohio. All quotations from Kirtland's lecture on tuberculosis are from this source.

9. Thomas Beddoes, M.D., and James Watt, engineer, *Considerations on the Medicinal Use and on the Production of Factitious Airs* (London: Bulgin and Rosser, 1795).

10. Jared Potter Kirtland to Sarah Boardman, 10 October 1851, In *Letters Written by Dr. Jared Potter Kirtland February 8, 1850 to June 27, 1853,* transcribed by Harold T. Clark, Archives of the Allen Medical Library, Health Sciences Library, Case Western Reserve University, Cleveland, Ohio.

11. Editorial, Jared Potter Kirtland. *Cleveland Medical Gazette.* November 1890, pp 26-39.

12. Charles J. B. Williams, *Op. cit.*

13. Jared Potter Kirtland, Handwritten lecture notes, Kirtland Collection, *Op. cit.*

14. Jared Potter Kirtland to C. Smith, M.D., 2 February 1852. In *Letters Written by Dr. Jared Potter Kirtland February 8, 1850 to June 27, 1853,* transcribed by Harold T. Clark, Archives of the Allen Medical Library, Health Sciences Library, Case Western Reserve University, Cleveland, Ohio.

15. Jared Potter Kirtland to Dr. John Andrews 15 October 1851, In *Letters Written by Dr. Jared Potter Kirtland February 8, 1850 to June 27, 1853,* transcribed by Harold T. Clark, Archives of the Allen Medical Library, Health Sciences Library, Case Western Reserve University, Cleveland, Ohio.

16. Jared Potter Kirtland to Mrs. Mary Ann Riddle, 29 May 1854, In *Letters Written by Dr. Jared Potter Kirtland February 8, 1850 to June 27, 1853,* transcribed by Harold T. Clark, Archives of the Allen Medical Library, Health Sciences Library, Case Western Reserve University, Cleveland, Ohio.

17. Jared Potter Kirtland to Dr. John Andrews 15 October 1851. *Op. cit.*
18. Jared Potter Kirtland to Mrs. Mary Malcolm 18 February 1850, In *Letters Written by Dr. Jared Potter Kirtland February 8, 1850 to June 27, 1853*, transcribed by Harold T. Clark, Archives of the Allen Medical Library, Health Sciences Library, Case Western Reserve University, Cleveland, Ohio.
19. Jared Potter Kirtland to Prof. Cassels 17 July 1856, In *Letters Written by Dr. Jared Potter Kirtland February 8, 1850 to June 27, 1853*, transcribed by Harold T. Clark, Archives of the Allen Medical Library, Health Sciences Library, Case Western Reserve University, Cleveland, Ohio.
20. Jared Potter Kirtland To C. Smith, 8 February 1852, In *Letters Written by Dr. Jared Potter Kirtland February 8, 1850 to June 27, 1853*, transcribed by Harold T. Clark, Archives of the Allen Medical Library, Health Sciences Library, Case Western Reserve University, Cleveland, Ohio.
21. Jared Potter Kirtland to Prof. J. Delamater, 19 July, 1856, In *Letters Written by Dr. Jared Potter Kirtland April 12, 1854 to August 1, 1856*, transcribed by Harold T. Clark, Archives of the Allen Medical Library, Health Sciences Library, Case Western Reserve University, Cleveland, Ohio.
22. Frederick Clayton Waite, *Western Reserve University Centennial History of the School of Medicine* (Cleveland, OH: Western Reserve University Press, 1946).
23. Works Projects Administration in Ohio, *Annals of Cleveland—1818-1935. Vol. 33. Abstracts from the Cleveland Herald. January 1 to December 31, 1847, abstract 628*, 1937.
24. Works Projects Administration in Ohio, *Annals of Cleveland—1818-1935. Vol. 33. Abstracts from the Daily True Democrat. January 1 to December 31, 1850, abstracts 1263-67*, 1937.
25. *Medical Fee Table of the City of Cleveland, Ohio* (Cleveland, OH: Bemis' Job Printing Establishment, undated). Exhibited at the Dittrick Center for Medical History, Case Western Reserve University, Cleveland, OH. Patsy Gerstner, *Looking for a Healthy Cleveland, 1810-1960*. (Cleveland, OH: Western Reserve Historical Society, 1998.)
26. *An Act to Incorporate Medical Societies for the Purpose of Regulating the Practice of Physic and Surgery in Ohio Together with the Proceedings of the General Medical Society*. (Columbus: Olmstead, Bailche and Camron, 1829).
27, E. B. Stevens, "A Historical Review of the Medical Association in Ohio," reported in Works Projects Administration in Ohio, *Annals of Cleveland— 1818-1935. Vol. 53. Abstracts from the Cleveland Leader. January 1, to December 31, 1870, abstract 2650*, 1937.
28. *Ibid.* Works Projects Administration in Ohio, *Annals of Cleveland—1818-1935. Vol. 52. Abstracts from the Cleveland Leader. January 1, to December 31, 1870, abstract 1089*, 1937. Works Projects Administration in Ohio, *An-*

nals of Cleveland—1818-1935. Vol. 34. Abstracts from the Daily True Democrat. January 1, to December 31, 1851, abstract 1232, 1937. Frederick C. Waite, "Jared Potter Kirtland: The Sage of Rockport," In Howard Dittrick, *Pioneer Medicine in the Western Reserve* (Cleveland, OH: The Academy of Medicine of Cleveland, 1932).

29. "1824-1926. Historical Summary of Organized Medicine in Cuyahoga County," *The Bulletin of the Academy of Medicine of Cleveland, Ohio* 10, no. 6 (1926):1-5, 16.

30. John S. Newberry, "Memoir of Jared Potter Kirtland. 1793-1877," Read before the National Academy, April 18, 1879. In *National Academy of Sciences. Biographical Memoirs. Vol. II* (Washington, DC: The Academy, 1886).

Chapter 9. Rockport. Pages 107-126.

1. Jared Potter Kirtland to Samuel P. Hildreth 7 December 1840, Archives of the Cleveland Museum of Natural History. Copy deposited by Margaret Manor Butler in 1980.

2. Jared Potter Kirtland, *Biographical Sketch of Dr. Jared Potter Kirtland Probably Dictated by Him an Age 81.* Copy deposited in the Archives of the Cleveland Museum of Natural History by Margaret Manor Butler in 1980.

3. Jared Potter Kirtland to Dr. S. P. Hildreth 28 September 1837, Archives of the Cleveland Museum of Natural History. Copy deposited by Margaret Manor Butler in 1980.

4. Jared Potter Kirtland to Samuel P. Hildreth 18 June 1839. Transcript deposited in the Archives of the Cleveland Museum of Natural History by Margaret Maron Butler in 1980.

5. Jared Potter Kirtland to Eliza S. Potter 27 August 1867. Archives of the Cleveland Museum of Natural History. Copy deposited by Margaret Manor Butler in 1980.

6. *Western Reserve Horticultural Review,* quoted in Works Projects Administration in Ohio, *Annals of Cleveland—1818-1935. Vol. 29. Abstracts from the Daily True Democrat. January 1 to December 31, 1851, Abstract 468,* 1937.

7. Works Projects Administration in Ohio, *Annals of Cleveland—1818-1935. Vol. 25. Abstracts from the Cleveland Herald. January 1 to December 31, 1842, Abstract 1161,* 1937.

8. Jared Potter Kirtland to Mr. Ellwanger 24 January 1853, In *Letters Written by Dr. Jared Potter Kirtland February 8, 1850 to June 27, 1853,* transcribed by Harold T. Clark, Archives of the Allen Medical Library, Health Sciences Library, Case Western Reserve University, Cleveland, Ohio.

9. *Ibid.*

10. Jared Potter Kirtland to Messrs, Hovey & Co. 4 February 1853. In *Letters Written by Dr. Jared Potter Kirtland February 8, 1850 to June 27, 1853,* tran-

scribed by Harold T. Clark, Archives of the Allen Medical Library, Health Sciences Library, Case Western Reserve University, Cleveland, Ohio.

11. Jared Potter Kirtland, "Artificial Manures," Western Reserve Magazine of Agriculture and Horticulture 1 (1845):147.

12. Jared P. Kirtland, M.D., "An Address, Delivered Before the Oberlin Agricultural and Horticultural Society, October 1st, 1845," Western Reserve Magazine of Agriculture and Horticulture 1 (1845): 220-35.

13. Jared P. Kirtland, "On the Selection of Locations, Favorable for Productive Orchards in Northern Ohio," Western Reserve Magazine of Agriculture and Horticulture 1 (1845):28, 25-29.

14. Works Projects Administration in Ohio, Annals of Cleveland—1818-1935. Vol. 43, Abstracts from the Cleveland Leader. January 1 to December 31, 1860, Abstract 708, 1937.

15. Works Projects Administration in Ohio, Annals of Cleveland—1818-1935. Vol. 42. Abstracts from the Cleveland Leader. January 1 to December 31, Abstract 1859, 1937.

16. Works Projects Administration in Ohio, Annals of Cleveland—1818-1935. Vol. 44. Abstracts from the Cleveland Leader. January 1 to December 31, 1861, Abstract 102, 1937.

17. Jared Potter Kirtland to Mr. Morgan 1 August 1856, In Letters Written by Dr. Jared Potter Kirtland April 12, 1854, to August 1, 1856, transcribed by Harold T. Clark, Archives of the Allen Medical Library, Health Sciences Library, Case Western Reserve University, Cleveland, Ohio.

18. Randolph C. Downes, History of Lake Shore Ohio: Vol. 1 (New York, NY: Lewis Historical Publishing Company, Inc., 1952). Jared Potter Kirtland, Biographical Sketch of Dr. Jared Potter Kirtland Probably Dictated by Him at Age 81. Op. cit. Kirtland's draft memoir gives the date of this visit as 1840, but the 1842 date is probably correct.

19. Jared Potter Kirtland to P.R. Hoy, M.D. 5 January 1855, In Letters Written by Dr. Jared Potter Kirtland April 12, 1854, to August 1, 1856, transcribed by Harold T. Clark. Archives of the Allen Medical Library, Health Sciences Library, Case Western Reserve University, Cleveland, Ohio.

20. Works Projects Administration in Ohio, Annals of Cleveland—1818-1935. Vol. 2, Abstracts from the Cleveland Herald. January 1 to December 31, 1842, Abstracts 1527 and 1528, 1937.

21. Jared Potter Kirtland to Miss Lizzie S. Potter 1 January 1868, Archives of the Cleveland Museum of Natural History. Copy deposited by Margaret Manor Butler in 1980.

22. Kirtland Family, Archives of the Mahoning Valley Historical Society, Collection 64, Box 17, File 88.32.15.01.01-88.32.15.01.07.

23. Jared Potter Kirtland, Biographical Sketch of Dr. Jared Potter Kirtland Probably Dictated by Him at Age 81. Op. cit.

24. Works Projects Administration in Ohio, *Annals of Cleveland—1818-1935*. *Vol. 25. Abstracts from the Daily Cleveland Herald. January 1 to December 31, 1842, abstract 1527*, 1937.

25. Works Projects Administration in Ohio, *Annals of Cleveland—1818-1935*. *Vol. 31. Abstracts from the Daily True Democrat. January 1 to December 31, 1848, Abstract 1205*, 1937.

26. Jared Potter Kirtland to Dr. John Andrews 15 October 1851, In *Letters Written by Dr. Jared Potter Kirtland February 8, 1850 to June 27, 1853*, transcribed by Harold T. Clark, Archives of the Allen Medical Library, Health Sciences Library, Case Western Reserve University, Cleveland, Ohio. The Christiana and Syracuse High Treason events to which Kirtland refers were episodes involving citizen attempts to succor fugitive slaves in Pennsylvania and New York.

27. Jared Potter Kirtland to Respected Relative 9 November 1855, In *Letters Written by Dr. Jared Potter Kirtland April 12, 1854, to August 1, 1856*, transcribed by Harold T. Clark, Archives of the Allen Medical Library, Health Sciences Library, Case Western Reserve University, Cleveland, Ohio.

28. Jared Potter Kirtland to Grant Toucey, M.D. 7 January 1855, In *Letters Written by Dr. Jared Potter Kirtland April 12, 1854, to August 1, 1856*, transcribed by Harold T. Clark, Archives of the Allen Medical Library, Health Sciences Library, Case Western Reserve University, Cleveland, Ohio.

29. Jared Potter Kirtland to Hon. S. P. Chase 5 March 1855, In *Letters Written by Dr. Jared Potter Kirtland April 12, 1854, to August 1, 1856*, transcribed by Harold T. Clark, Archives of the Allen Medical Library, Health Sciences Library, Case Western Reserve University, Cleveland, Ohio.

30. Jared Potter Kirtland to Sarah Kirtland 8 February 1853, In *Letters Written by Dr. Jared Potter Kirtland February 8, 1850 to June 27, 1853*, transcribed by Harold T. Clark, Archives of the Allen Medical Library, Health Sciences Library, Case Western Reserve University, Cleveland, Ohio.

31. Jared Potter Kirtland to Dr. S. P. Hildreth 28 February 1837. Jared Potter Kirtland to Dr. S. P. Hildreth 28 September 1837. Archives of the Cleveland Museum of Natural History. Copies deposited by Margaret Manor Butler in 1980.

32. Jared Potter Kirtland to Dr. S. P. Hildreth, 28 September 1837. *Op. cit.*

33. Jared Potter Kirtland to Dr. Hubbard 11 April 1853, Archives of the Cleveland Museum of Natural History. Copy deposited by Margaret Manor Butler in 1980.

34. Jared Potter Kirtland to Samuel P. Hildreth 11 November 1850, Archives of the Cleveland Museum of Natural History. Copy deposited by Margaret Manor Butler in 1980.

35. Jared Potter Kirtland to Dr. S. P. Hildreth 11 April 1835, Archives of the Cleveland Museum of Natural History. Copy deposited by Margaret Manor Butler in 1980.

36. Jared Potter Kirtland to Robt Thompson, M.D. 10 February 1850, In *Letters Written by Dr. Jared Potter Kirtland February 8, 1850 to June 27, 1853*, transcribed by Harold T. Clark, Archives of the Allen Medical Library, Health Sciences Library, Case Western Reserve University, Cleveland, Ohio.
37. Jared Potter Kirtland to Respected Cousin [Sarah Potter Carrington] 13 July 1854, In *Letters Written by Dr. Jared Potter Kirtland April 12, 1854 to August 1, 1856*, transcribed by Harold T. Clark, Archives of the Allen Medical Library, Health Sciences Library, Case Western Reserve University, Cleveland, Ohio.
38. Jared Potter Kirtland to Dear Mary, undated letter probably written in August 1854. In *Letters Written by Dr. Jared Potter Kirtland April 12, 1854, to August 1, 1856*, transcribed by Harold T. Clark, Archives of the Allen Medical Library, Health Sciences Library, Case Western Reserve University, Cleveland, Ohio.
39. Jared Potter Kirtland to C. W. Fitch 26 July 1854, In *Letters Written by Dr. Jared Potter Kirtland April 12, 1854, to August 1, 1856*, transcribed by Harold T. Clark, Archives of the Allen Medical Library, Health Sciences Library, Case Western Reserve University, Cleveland, Ohio.
40. Jared Potter Kirtland to Mary Potter Hall 27 December 1852, In *Letters Written by Dr. Jared Potter Kirtland February 8, 1850 to June 27, 1853*, transcribed by Harold T. Clark, Archives of the Allen Medical Library, Health Sciences Library, Case Western Reserve University, Cleveland, Ohio.
41. Jared Potter Kirtland to Respected Friend 12 July 1854. Transcript deposited in the Archives of the Cleveland Museum of Natural History by Margaret Manor Butler in 1980.
42. *Ibid.*
43. "Editorial," *The Family Visitor* (3 January 1850):4.
44. Jared Potter Kirtland to Miss Lizzie S. Potter 18 October 1866. Transcript deposited in the Archives of the Cleveland Museum of Natural History by Margaret Manor Butler in 1980.
45. Jared Potter Kirtland, "Disasters Attending the Expeditions of Major Wilkins, and Colonel (Afterwards General) Bradstreet, Near the Present City of Cleveland," In Charles Whittlesey, *Early History of Cleveland, Ohio, Including Original Papers and Other Matter Relating to the Adjacent Country* (Fairbanks, Benedict & Co.: Cleveland, OH, 1867).
46. "Professor Jared Potter Kirtland, LLD," *Magazine of Western History* 2 (1885):7681. Copies of this correspondence, which is quoted in this published tribute, do not exist in any of the several archives containing Kirtland letters searched by the author.
47. *Ibid.*
48. *Ibid.*
49. Omar Ranney, "Name of Dr. Kirtland, Pioneer Cleveland Scientist, Is Still Famous Here," *Cleveland Press*, 18 January 1941.

Bibliography of Published Works Cited

Books

Aley, Howard C. *A Heritage to Share: The Bicentennial History of Youngstown and Mahoning County, Ohio*. Youngstown, OH: The Bicentennial Commission of Youngstown and Mahoning County, Ohio, 1975.

Anderson, Robert Charles. *The Great Migration. Immigrants to New England. 1634-1635. Volume IV*. Boston, MA: New England Historic Genealogical Society, 2005.

Beddoes, Thomas, and James Watt. *Considerations on the Medicinal Use and on the Production of Factitious Airs*. London: Bulgin and Rosser, 1795.

Boorstin, Daniel J. *The Americans: The Colonial Experience*. New York, NY: Vintage Books, 1958.

Breen, T. H. *Puritans and Adventurers. Change and Persistence in Early America*. New York, NY: Oxford University Press, 1980.

Cochrane, Rexmond C. *The National Academy of Sciences: The First Hundred Years: 1863-1963*. Washington, DC: National Academy of Sciences, 1978.

Collyer, R. H. *Manual of Phrenology or the Physiology of the Human Brain Embracing a Full Description of the Phrenological Organs, their Exact Location, and the Peculiarities of Character Produced by their Various Degrees of Development and Combination*. Cincinnati, OH: Alexander Flash, 1838.

Davis, Charles Henry Stanley. *History of Wallingford, Conn. From its Settlement in 1670 to the Present Time, Including Meriden, which was one of its Parishes until 1806, and Cheshire, which was Incorporated in 1780*. Meriden, CT: Published by the Author, 1870.

Dean, John Ward, ed. *Historical and Genealogical Register. Vol. XLVIII. 1894*. Bowie, MD: Heritage Books, Inc., 1997.

Dittrick, Howard. *Pioneer Medicine in the Western Reserve*. Cleveland, OH: The Academy of Medicine of Cleveland, 1932.

Downes, Randolph C. *History of Lake Shore Ohio*. New York, NY: Lewis Historical Publishing Company, Inc., 1952.

Ferguson, Thomas E. *Ohio Lands. A Short History. Third Edition.* Columbus, OH: Ohio Auditor of State, 1991.

Fischer, David Hackett. *Albion's Seed. Four British Folkways in America.* New York, NY: Oxford University Press, 1989.

Flexner, Abraham. *Medical Education in the United States and Canada: A Report to the Carnegie Foundation for the Advancement of Teaching: With an Introduction by Henry S. Pritchett.* New York, NY: Carnegie Foundation for the Advancement of Teaching, 1910.

Flexner, James Thomas. *Doctors on Horseback. Pioneers of American Medicine.* New York: The Viking Press, 1937.

Gerstner, Patsy. *Looking for a Healthy Cleveland, 1810-1960.* Cleveland, OH: Western Reserve Historical Society, 1998.

Gilkey, Elliot Howard. *The Ohio Hundred Year Book. A Hand-Book of the Public Men and Public Institutions of Ohio from the Northwest Territory. 1787 to July 1, 1901.* Columbus, OH: Fred J. Heer, 1901.

Guess, Carl. *Ohio House of Representatives Membership Directory: 1803-1965/66.* Columbus, OH: Columbus Blank Book Co., 1966.

Hatcher, Harlan. *The Western Reserve. The Story of New Connecticut in Ohio.* Indianapolis, IN: The Bobbs-Merrill Company, Inc., 1949.

Haydn, Hiram Collins. *Western Reserve University from Hudson to Cleveland 1878-1890: An Historical Sketch.* Cleveland, OH: Western Reserve University, 1905.

Hayes, Thomas. *A Serious Address on the Dangerous Consequences of Neglecting Common Coughs and Colds with Ample Directions for the Prevention and Cure of Consumptions to which are Added Observations on the Hooping Cough and Asthma.* Boston, MA: Samuel Etheridge, 1796.

Hendrickson, Walter B. *The Arkites and Other Pioneer Natural History Organizations of Cleveland.* Cleveland, OH: The Press of Western Reserve University, 1962.

A History of the First Half-Century of the National Academy of Sciences: 1863-1913. Baltimore, MD: The Lord Baltimore Press, 1913.

History of Trumbull and Mahoning Counties with Illustrations and Biographical Sketches. Vol. I. Cleveland, OH: H.Z. Williams & Bro., 1882.

Hyde, Roberta Graves, Sally Bloomfield Mazer, and Barbara Houser Layfield, eds. *Trumbull County Ohio Marriage Record Index: One Hundred Years: 1800-1900: Volume I, A-M.* Cortland, OH: Howard Printing, 1998.

Izant, Grace Goulder. *Hudson's Heritage. A Chronicle of the Founding and Flowering of the Village of Hudson, Ohio.* Kent, OH: The Kent State University Press, 1985.

Joblin, Maurice. *Cleveland, Past and Present: Its Representative Men. Comprising Biographical Sketches of Pioneer Settlers and Prominent Citizens: With a History of the City and Historical Sketches of Its Commerce, Manufactures, Ship*

Building, Railroads, Telegraphy, Schools, Churches, Etc. Cleveland, OH: Fairbanks, Benedict & Co., Printers, 1869.

Kelley, Howard A. *A Cyclopedia of American Medical Biography Comprising the Lives of Eminent Deceased Physicians and Surgeons from 1610 to 1910. Vol. II.* Philadelphia, PA: W.B. Saunders Company, 1912.

Kennedy, James Harrison. *A History of the City of Cleveland, Its Settlement and Progress, 1796-1896.* Cleveland, OH: The Imperial Press, 1896.

Kirtland, Charles A. *The Kirtland Family, or, the Descendants of John and Lydia Pratt Kirtland: Who Were Among the First Settlers of Saybrook.* Deep River, CT: Charles A. Kirtland, 1930.

Kirtland, Jared P. *Introductory Lecture on the Coinciding Tendencies of Medicines.* Cleveland, OH: Steam Press of M.C. Younglove & Co., 1848.

Kirtland, Turhand. *Diary of Turhand Kirtland from 1798-1800. While Surveying and Laying Out the Western Reserve for the Connecticut Land Company.* Poland, OH: Mary L.W. Morse, 1903.

Laennec, René T. H. *A Treatise on the Disease of the Chest in which they are Described According to their Anatomical Characters, and their Diagnosis Established on a New Principle by Means of Acoustick Instruments.* Translated by John Forbes. London: T. and G. Underwood, 1821.

Lupold, Harry F., and Gladys Haddad, eds. *Ohio's Western Reserve. A Regional Reader.* Kent, OH: The Kent State University Press, 1988.

Mahoning Valley Historical Society. *Historical Collections of the Mahoning Valley Containing an Account of the Two Pioneer Reunions: Together with a Selection of Interesting Facts, Traditions, Biographical Sketches, Anecdotes, Etc., Relating to the Sales and Settlement of the Lands Belonging to the Connecticut Land Company and History and Reminiscences, Both General and Local. Vol. I.* Youngstown, OH: Mahoning Valley Historical Society, 1990.

Mather, William W. *First Annual Report of the Geological Survey of the State of Ohio.* Columbus, OH: Samuel Medary, Printer to the State, 1838.

McMahon, Bernard. *The American Gardener's Calendar; Adapted to the Climates and Seasons of the United States.* Philadelphia, PA: B. Graves, 1806.

Nathan, Jean. *Ohio Marriages Recorded in County Courts: 1 Jan 1821-31-Dec 1830: An Index.* Mansfield, OH: The Ohio Genealogical Society, 2003.

Ohio State Board of Agriculture. *The Farmers' Centennial History of Ohio 1803-1903.* Springfield, OH: The Springfield Publishing Company, State Printers, 1904.

Proceedings of the American Association for the Advancement of Science: First Meeting, Held at Philadelphia September, 1848. Philadelphia, PA: John C. Clark, 1849.

Rafinesque, Constantine S. *Ichthyologia Ohiensis, or Natural History of the Fishes Inhabiting the River Ohio and its Tributary Streams.* Lexington, KY: W.G. Hunt, 1820.

Rice, Harvey. *Sketches of Western Reserve Life.* New York, NY: Lee and Shepard, 1888.

Say, Thomas. *American Conchology or Descriptions of the Shells of North America: Illustrated by Coloured Figures from Original Drawings Executed from Nature.* New Harmony, IN: School Press, 1830.

Sprague, William B. *Annals of the American Pulpit or Commemorative Notices of Distinguished American Clergymen of Various Denominations from the Early Settlement of the Country to the Close of the Year Eighteen Hundred and Fifty-five. Vol. V.* New York, NY: Robert Carter & Brothers, 1861.

Stokes, Anson Phelps. *Memorials of Eminent Yale Men: A Biographical Study of Student Life and University Influences During Eighteenth and Nineteenth Centuries. Vol. II. Science and Public Life.* New Haven, CT: Yale University Press, 1914.

Vital Records of Saybrook, 1647-1834. Hartford, CT: The Connecticut Historical Society & the Connecticut Society of the Order of Founders and Patriots of America, 1948.

Waite, Frederick Clayton. *Western Reserve University. The Hudson Era. A History of Western Reserve College and Academy at Hudson, Ohio, from 1826-1882.* Cleveland, OH: Western Reserve University Press, 1943.

Waite, Frederick Clayton. *Western Reserve University Centennial History of the School of Medicine.* Cleveland, OH: Western Reserve University Press, 1946.

Williams, Greer. *Western Reserve's Experiment in Medical Education and Its Outcome.* New York, NY: Oxford University Press, 1980.

Articles

Allen, Dudley P. "Pioneer medicine on the Western Reserve." *Magazine of Western History Illustrated* 4 (1886): 444-52.

Anderson, Russell H. "The Pease Map of the Connecticut Western Reserve." *The Ohio State Archaeological and Historical Quarterly* 63. (1954): 270-82.

Baker, Albert R., and Samuel W. Kelley. "Editorial." *Cleveland Medical Gazette* 6. (1890): 3-39.

Cassels, J. Lang. "Notice of a Meteorite Which Fell in Hindustan in 1857." *American Journal of Science* 32, no. 96. (1861): 51-53.

Coover, A. B. "Ohio Banking Institutions, 1803-1866." *Ohio Archaeological and Historical Publications* 21. (1912): 296-320.

Curtis, George M. "Jared Potter Kirtland, M.D., 'The sage of Rockport,' November 10, 1793-December 18, 1877." *The Ohio State Archaeological and Historical Quarterly* 50. (1941): 326-37.

Curtis, George M. "Jared Potter Kirtland, M.D.: Pioneer Naturalist of the Western Reserve: November 10, 1793-December 18, 1877." *Ohio State Medical Journal* 37. 1941:971-77.

"Editorial." *The Family Visitor.* (3 January 1850): 4.

Fertig, Henry H. "Some Letters of Jared Potter Kirtland." *Ohio State Medical Journal* 51. (1955): 553-57.

Franklin, Benjamin. "A Plan for Settling Two Western Colonies, 1755." Reproduced in Wheeler, Robert A., ed., *Visions of the Western Reserve. Public and Private Documents of Northeastern Ohio, 1750-1860.* Columbus, OH: Ohio State University Press, 2000.

Gehr, Agnes Robbins. "Jared Potter Kirtland." *The Explorer* 2, no. 7. (1952): 1-33.

Gerstner, Patsy A. "The Personality of Jared Potter Kirtland as Revealed by Phrenology." *Bulletin of the Cleveland Medical Library* 18. (1971): 60-63.

Gifford, G. Edmund, Jr. "Doctors Afield: Dr. Jared Kirtland and His Warbler." *New England Journal of Medicine* 287 (1972): 909-11.

Grigg, E. R. N. "The Arcana of Tuberculosis with a Brief Epidemiologic History of the Disease in the U.S.A. Part III. Epidemiologic History of Tuberculosis in the United States." *American Review of Tuberculosis and Pulmonary Disease* 78. (1958): 426-53.

Kirtland, Jared Potter. "Observations on the Sexual Characters of the Animals Belonging to Lamarck's Family of *Naiades.*" *American Journal of Science and Arts* 26. (1834): 117-20.

Kirtland, Jared Potter. "Descriptions of Four New Species of Fishes." *Boston Journal of Natural History* 3. (1840-1841): 273-77.

Kirtland, Jared Potter. "Descriptions of the Fishes of the Ohio River and its Tributaries." *Boston Journal of Natural History* 3. (1840-1841): 338-52; 3. (1840-1841): 469-82; 4. (1843-1844): 15-26; 4. (1843-1844): 231-40; 4. (1843-1844): 303-08; 5. (1845-1847): 21-32; 5. (1845-1847): 265-76; 5. (1845-1847): 330-34.

Kirtland, Jared P. "On the Selection of Locations, Favorable for Productive Orchards in Northern Ohio." *Western Reserve Magazine of Agriculture and Horticulture* 1. (1845): 2-8, 25-29.

Kirtland, Jared P. "An Address, Delivered Before the Oberlin Agricultural and Horticultural Society, October 1st, 1845." *Western Reserve Magazine of Agriculture and Horticulture* 1. (1845): 220-35.

Kirtland, Jared Potter. "Peculiarities of Climate, Flora and Fauna of the South Shore of Lake Erie in the Vicinity of Cleveland, Ohio." *American Journal of Science and the Arts* 13. (1852): 215-19.

Kirtland, Jared Potter. "Disasters Attending the Expeditions of Major Wilkins, and Colonel. Afterwards General Bradstreet, Near the Present City of Cleveland." In *Early History of Cleveland, Ohio, Including Original Papers and Other Matter Relating to the Adjacent Country*, by Charles Whittlesey. Fairbanks, Benedict & Co.: Cleveland, OH, 1867.

Large, John, Jr. "A Scientist Observes Florida: 1870." *Florida Historical Quarterly* 42. (1963): 48-54.

Newberry, J. S., "Memoir of Jared Potter Kirtland, 1793-1877." *National Academy of Sciences: Bibliographical Memoirs: Vol. II.* Washington, DC: The Academy, 1886.

Orth, Samuel P. "Appendix." In *A History of Cleveland Ohio with Numerous Chapters by Special Contributors. Vol. I.* Cleveland, OH: The S. J. Clarke Publishing Co., 1910.

Ranney, Omar, "Name of Dr. Kirtland, Pioneer Cleveland Scientist, Is Still Famous Here." *Cleveland Press*, Jan. 18, 1941.

Rogers, Rebecca M., "Dr Jared P. Kirtland: Amateur of Horticulture." *Journal of Garden History* 6. 1986:357-75.

Stokstad, Erik. "Nearly Buried, Mussels Get a Helping Hand." *Science* 338. (2012): 876-78.

Waite, Frederick C. "Jared Potter Kirtland—physician, teacher, scientist." *Bulletin of the Cleveland Academy of Medicine* 14, no. 7. (1930): 5-6.

Waite, Frederick C. "John Delamater, educator and physician, founder of the School of Medicine of Western Reserve University." *Bulletin of the Academy of Medicine of Cleveland* 14, no 5. (1930): 9-10, 18, 20.

Waite, Frederick C. "Jared Potter Kirtland. Physician, Teacher, Horticulturist, and Eminent Naturalist." *Ohio Journal of Science* 30. (1930): 153-68.

Waite, Frederick C. "Jared Potter Kirtland: The Sage of Rockport." In *Pioneer Medicine in the Western Reserve*, edited by Howard Dittrick. Cleveland, OH: The Academy of Medicine of Cleveland, 1932.

Waite, Frederick C. "Medical Education in Ohio." *Ohio State Medical Journal* 49. (1953): 623-26.

Wheeler, Robert A. "The Connecticut Generis of the Western Reserve." *Ohio History* 114. (2007): 57-78.

Wilson, Ella Grant. "Dr. Jared P. Kirtland." *Cleveland Plain Dealer*, Oct. 18, 1931.

Index

Chase, Samuel P., 118
Cherries, Jared Potter Kirtland's varieties of, 41-42, 109-110
Cheshire Academy, 29-30
Cholera, 80, 101-2, 120-21; in Cleveland, 80, 102, 120
Cincinnati College Medical Department. *See* Ohio College of Medicine in Cincinnati
Civil War, Jared Potter Kirtland and, 117, 118
Clark, Sir James, 99
Clarke, Nancy, 67
Cleaveland, Moses, 16-17, 127
Cleveland, Ohio, 16-18, 21, 32, 50; Jared Potter Kirtland and drinking water for, 102, 132; Jared Potter Kirtland's house in, 57, 60, 107, 109, 131
Cleveland Academy of Medicine. *See* Academy of Medicine of Cleveland
Cleveland Academy of Natural Science, 77, 83-85, 131, 133; Jared Potter Kirtland president of, 83, 85, 131, 133; proceedings of, 77, 83, 84
Cleveland Horticultural Society, 110
Cleveland and Pittsburgh Railroad Company, 108
Cleveland Medical College. *See* Western Reserve College, Medical Department of
Cleveland Museum of Natural History, 83, 85, 133, 134; Kirtland Bird Club and, 85; Kirtlandia Society and, 85, 134
Collyer, Robert H., 51-54
Conchology. *See* molluscs
Connecticut, borders of, 13-15, 127; Western Reserve of. *See* Western Reserve of Connecticut
Connecticut Land Company, 11, 16, 21, 25-26, 127
Consumption. *See* tuberculosis
Cutter, Caroline Pease, 89

Cutter, Kelsey, 86
Cuyahoga River, 16, 17-18, 22, 23
Darwin, Charles, 81-82
Delamater, Jacob J., 63, 66, 103-4
Delamater, John, 43, 59-61, 63, 65, 89, 103-5, 130, 131
Diarrheal disease, 120; Jared Potter Kirtland's treatment of, 100-102
Drake, Daniel, 48, 49-50, 56-57
Durham, Connecticut, 38-39, 51, 129
Elliott, Henry W., 85
Ellwanger's Nursery, 110
Erysipelas, Jared Potter Kirtland afflicted by, 121
Fairfield Medical College, 43, 58, 59, 60
Family Visitor, The, 122-23, 132
Firelands, 15, 127
Fish, of Lake Erie, 32; of Ohio, 74-75, 76-79, 123, 130
Fitch, Zalmon, 44
Flexner, Abraham, 68; report of, 68, 133
Florida, Jared Potter Kirtland's travel to, 86, 133
Fowler, Jonathan, 20-21, 127
Franklin, William, 27-29
Garlick, Theodatus, 125-26
Goforth, William, 49, 56-57
Grand River, 11, 19, 128
Hayes, Thomas, 93-94, 96
Hildreth, Samuel P., 73, 75, 107
Hippocrates, 55
Home League, Jared Potter Kirtland and, 114
Homeopathic Medical Schools in Ohio, 67
Homeopathy, Jared Potter Kirtland's views of, 88
Hopewell (ship carrying immigrants to North America), 8, 9
Hudson, Ohio, 23-24, 61, 128
Hudson, David, Jr., 22-24, 61-62, 128
Hydrotherapy, 56, 88
Johnson, Parnel, 7, 10

Index

About the Author

Thomas M. Daniel, M.D., is Professor Emeritus of Medicine at Case Western University and Honorary Physician at University Hospitals of Cleveland. He is a graduate of Yale University and Harvard Medical School, and is board-certified in internal medicine and pulmonary disease.

During his academic career, Dr. Daniel was a member of the pulmonary medicine division at University Hospitals of Cleveland and an active teacher of medical students and medical residents. He directed a research laboratory studying immune responses to tuberculosis. Dr. Daniel served on numerous national committees related to pulmonary medicine, especially tuberculosis. Since retirement, he has focused on medical history and has published numerous medical history articles in scientific journals and six previous books, among them *Times and Tides of Tuberculosis*, Fithian Press, 2013, and *Captain of Death: The Story of ˙ ˀrculosis*, University of Rochester Press, 1997.